Broken Bread

A Gastronomic Journey Into Healing

*A memoir as told by
a wee tad bit of a wreck*

Colette Ledoux

BROKEN BREAD

A Gastronomic Journey Into Healing

ISBN: 978-1-9992637-0-6

broken-bread.ca

Design by Transcendent Publishing

Author photo by Chris Walkling

Printed in the United States of America.

This book is dedicated to

Claude

Also dedicated to my memory

*It's taken me so long to finish this "little" project,
I could recite it backwards!*

"May the tapestry be versatile — a tablecloth to welcome company or a comforter to soothe my rattled nerves."

~Colette

Contents

Preface xi
Introduction.. xiii
Part One: Threading the Needle...................................... xvii
Vignette 1 1
Vignette 2 9
Vignette 3 17
Vignette 4 29
    Mother's Scrambled Eggs.................................35
    GF Yorkshire Pudding 36
    Dad's Chili 37
    Browned Flour for Gravy 39
    My Kitchen Staples 41
Vignette 5 49
    GF Bread 57
    Brazilian Queijo Buns 59
    Queijo Pizza Crust 61
    Queijo Appetizers...61
    Grace's Italian Butter.....................................62
    GF French Bread 63
Vignette 6 67
Vignette 7 75
    Aunt Dot's Salmon Patties 83
    Homemade Mayo..83
    Aunt Hazel's Wonderful Tea Biscuits 85
    Spinach Salad 86
    Pasta Sauce 86
    Meatballs...88
    Baked Eggplant – Non-Breaded.....................91
    Veal or Chicken Scallopini 93

Veal, Chicken or Eggplant Parmesan 95
Spicy Summer Cannellini Beans & Sausage ...98
My Alternative Pasta Sauce 100
Vignette 8 103
Vignette 9 113
Traditions...119
Mémère's Christmas Holiday Serving
Guide 121
Sea Pie – Cipaille...122
Ledoux Ragout - Pork Meatballs in Gravy ...126
Tourtière - Meat Pie....................................130
GF Pie Crust..133
Turkey 135
Gravy for Traditional Oven-Roasted Turkey137
Stuffing...138
Stuffing Made Outside the Turkey Cavity....140
Grandma Lorna Walkling's Cranberry
Sauce 141
Nana's Carrots 141
Nana's Mashed Potatoes 142
Morning Potatoes...143
The Humble Christmas Salad 144
Christmas Cocktail Meatballs 145
Bouillée...147
My Old-Fashioned Baked Beans 150
Simple Kick-Ass Barbeque Sauce 152
Hearty Pureed Vegetable & Crispy Parsnip
Soup 153
Dessert..156
Butter Tarts 156
Classic Crème Brûlée....................................158
Part Two: Learning to Weave 161
Vignette 10...163

Vignette 11 171

Vignette 12 181

Vignette 13 189

Vignette 14 193

    George's Prime Rib of Beef 196

    Beef Bourguignon 198

    Coq Au Vin 200

    Barbequed Rack of Lamb 203

Vignette 15 205

Part Three: Every Tapestry Needs a Border 215

Vignette 16 217

Vignette 17 221

Vignette 18 225

Vignette 19 241

A Few More Words 247

Personal Observations 255

Glossary 261

References 269

Preface

Discovering that writing was my *raison d'être* filled me with a rare sense of exuberance. There was an intoxicating whiff in the air that could only be perceived as the sweet scent of success. I've never attempted a summersault, but there's no doubt that, with my newfound level of confidence, I easily could've done cartwheels on a tightrope.

The itch to write non-stop had convinced me that it was reasonable to expect this writing exercise could be wrapped up in a matter of weeks. This notion, I believed, was further evidenced by my adoption of certain habits often assigned to seasoned writers. My fingers felt agile as they caressed the computer keys, expeditiously, and I began keeping hours akin to bats and badgers, thinking that burning midnight oil would ensure a timely completion.

I'd blush with pride when reciting the freshly quarried words to my husband Claude, using as much theatrical flourish as I could muster. Bless his patient, foolish heart, as he sat, intently listening to my daily matinee, while barely noticing the changing of seasons. The reading always started from the first page, ensuring the words were forever dedicated to memory.

The year the writing began was 2010.

2020 has now been ushered in, and it's hard to believe how quickly time has passed or how my writing breaks morphed from short afternoon siestas into lengthy retreats. Though I'm a bit off schedule, it's lovely to finally be here, with my mission complete, sharing my story with you.

Introduction

Each spring, a new assortment of robins' nests will appear in the cubby holes created by the crossbeams under my deck. Once a robin has claimed her territory, she ingeniously goes about building her nest by weaving together peculiar odds and ends. The scavenged remnants seem absurdly out of place, but each strand of "this and that" is needed to reinforce the strength of her unique little structure. Much like a robin, in order to structure the following narrative, I've needed to weave together an oddball assortment of threads – some frayed, and some old.

The roots of the narrative begin in Toronto's Little Italy of the 1960s. I've always assumed there were only two notable takeaways from the experience: one was daring to say, as a properly raised Catholic girl, the forbidden expletive vaffanculo (I pronounced it vafungula), a word that anyone who knew it meant fuck off (mi scusi for swearing) didn't appreciate hearing; the other was my diehard love of Italian food.

I'm not of Italian heritage, but as an observant kid, maybe even a bit nosy, I was uniquely positioned to admire the *signoras and nonnas* as they bustled about preparing delectable feasts – feasts where angels played harps when apron strings rustled. The most treasured memories of my childhood were the countless times I was fortunate enough to be present at their dinner tables, and I never imagined the day would come when I'd no longer be able to enjoy their food as it's traditionally prepared. As it turns out, my destiny, instead, would be that of a dandy collector of food-related autoimmune conditions.

My mind is contradictory by nature, a playground where devils and angels fight for turf, and I'm set in my ways, which made the prospect of easily conforming to lifestyle changes difficult. I mean the kind of *difficult* a diehard vegan with a broken jaw would have if forced to eat an all-beef hotdog, enticingly topped with turnip sprouts.

Good grief, to compound matters, I also live with nagging anxiety, and, until now, I've always been in bird-brained denial, carelessly preferring to ignore, instead of address, issues related to health. It's taken time, but surprisingly, I've discovered that a profound attitude change can happen. A marvelous revelation, indeed!

My wish is that you'll find something useful in this collection of eclectic vignettes, threaded together with a sprinkling of recipes.

By Way of Introduction
Gathering the Threads of I's

You do not know me. I do not know myself, except for this:

*I'm wise. I move mountains. I'm foolish.
I make mountains out of tiny hills.*

*I'm open – but painfully shy. I swallowed the toothpick in my
bacon-wrapped filet mignon – I'd rather choke to death than
live to make a scene.*

I'm larger than life – but invisible.

I roar with laughter – while always on the verge of tears.

I'm lighthearted – but weighted with worry.

*I compliment warmly for gestures of kindness – but rarely
forgive and never forget.*

I'm blessed. No Evil Eye has cursed me yet.

*I was born in the Chinese Zodiac Year of the Pig – yet I'm
stubborn like a mule.*

*I'm a contradiction by nature. How could I not be? My Virgo
signs are the Goddess of Harvest with wheat sheaf in hand,
along with a sapphire stone.*

Part One

Threading the Needle

V.1

How fitting it was, to have this particular medical appointment scheduled for a frigid January day in 2007. It shouldn't be dramatically compared to the dreaded "frosty Friday in hell," but it at least deserved a forbidden *vaffanculo* reference. My now petite body, the result of months of illness and weight loss, had shed the protective layer of fat that had once provided it warmth, and with the long trek home, it wasn't a stretch to think my bones might crack from freezing. My coat from the previous winter could now be refashioned, with enough material left over to make a small area rug.

As I turned my gaze upward, forlornly, the clouds were beginning to resemble scattered piles of ice shards, and it wouldn't be long before the hues of cream and pink would be devoured by smoky grey. When dejectedly looking downward (visualize that famous old Hunchback), the stitching on my jacket's hem was visible. Once home, there was no need to put on my apron – what needed to be swallowed didn't involve food. There was only one sensible way to calm my rattled nerves, and a bottle of wine was uncorked.

The kitchen lighting was set to a soft glow to banish the late-day blanket of greyness that now clung like Saran wrap. With glass in hand, I stared out at the snow-covered pines and tangle of leaf-stripped nude maples beyond, that so aptly reflected my sentiment, which was nothing other than numb-ingly frozen.

The test result, which the gastroenterologist sympathetically stated he wouldn't want to live with, indicated the need for severe dietary restrictions, and acceptance would certainly necessitate a decent measure of grace. Surely, I'd be a shoo-in for admittance to The Promised Land under any circum-stance, but medical non-compliance could quite possibly hasten my arrival at the Pearly Gates and no doubt prompt an interview process. In this case, I'd either have to lie about my wayward behaviour (assuming such a thing was possible), or hope to find a decent spot in Purgatory. Searching for an epiphany to deal with my new reality would prove to be a tall order.

The consequences of a CD (celiac disease) diagnosis, and the life sentence of the preposterous, exacting GF (gluten-free) diet that was prescribed, couldn't be sugar-coated, especially since it followed an earlier diagnosis of MC (microscopic colitis). Verbalizing having "MC/CD" which requires a "GF" diet seemed absurd, more aptly suitable for describing acou-stic instruments needing batteries.

The specific culprit that defines CD is gluten, that won-derful combo of magical proteins found in some of the most familiar grains such as wheat, barley, and rye. It made me uncharacteristically crusty to think that everything was perfectly edible before I'd left for my doctor's appointment, and in a matter of hours most everything was toxic, even a crumb from a piece of bread – the staff of life, for God's sake!

Until now, the best days in life were the simple ones, where I'd putter in my kitchen in preparation of dinner, followed by the breaking of bread that signifies the familial time-honoured act of sharing a meal together. In the literal sense, bread is "broken" because it's a crime to slice a fresh baguette. Tearing it into chunks with my hands, with lots of gusto, is the best way to expose its unique nooks and crannies. The unfussy manner of serving it this way authenticates its value while enhancing the experience of eating it.

A positive biopsy confirmed that gluten was as lethal to my body as Kryptonite was to Superman's. The dietician warned that even a mere speck of gluten, so small it could sit on the head of a pin, would cause damage, so a harm-reduction strategy was out of the question. In other words, no damn cheating, *ever*. This assertion didn't line up with my unique, somewhat eccentric perspective. How could it, when I'd long suffered from a full-blown addiction to gluten-containing foods? After all, these were the delectable comfort foods, my favourite being Italian, that I perceived acted as a pacifier for an addled psyche. Given a chance to turn back the clock to the pre-diagnosis era, I'd have creatively used gluten to brush my teeth, followed by putting a dab behind my ears and on my wrists each morning.

In recent years, millions of people have come to believe that gluten is evil, some with a fervour akin to that of a religious movement. Who's to judge whether they're right or wrong when they claim that eating GF led them to their first

"Come to Jesus" moment? If they feel better, that's that. For me, in a state of utter panic over test results I was struggling to accept, it was "Say what?"

Little did I know that patiently waiting in the wings was another food-related condition preparing to make its stormy debut. When the storm arrived, it was snowing sugar.

Hearing the news of the Type II diabetes felt like being hit by an oversized snowball. A sweet tooth had never made my list of "not so good" traits, but it's funny how quickly I dreamed of sitting in a Paris pâtisserie, pretending I had a right to devour deadly, sinful, gluten-laden, sugary delights, like Jésuite pastry with almond cream. It would be a quaint little shop where the baker herself would tend to me. She'd be wearing a crisp black shirt beautifully embellished with a fine dusting of glutinous flour and icing sugar, speckles of it dotting her flushed, rosy cheeks. She'd see my delight when admiring her pretty creations and add a few complimentary Pets de Soeur (Nuns Farts) onto my plate. While blowing kisses, I'd promise to see her again someday – in another dream. "Je t'aime madame! Merci beaucoup!"

Of course, managing this condition wouldn't be a simple case of avoiding pretend French pastry, and I was once again presented with a laundry list of dietary restrictions. Given the exasperating task, I started imagining easier solutions, like surviving on a steady diet of seasoned dryer lint.

～

Avoiding a world infested with gluten wasn't my only priority. Chronic anxiety (my mind is dancing jitterbug when I'd prefer ballet) has veiled my entire existence, taking the lion's share of the blame for the heavy weight of the world that teeters on my shoulders. A sunny disposition disguises the affliction, although I've never tried to hide it because it's as much a part of me as having curly hair. Having this condition encompasses those near and dear, shapes my world view, and, sometimes to my detriment, affects how I treat myself.

As for those near and dear – my best intentions were never to cluck and coddle, but sensibility never allowed anyone in my orbit to roam free-range. My anxiety-ridden, protective tendencies are a bit baffling, considering that I was raised in a house where Mother couldn't shoo kids out of the house fast enough. Without fail she'd ship my sister and me up the street to the church on Saturday afternoons to "attend" the wedding ceremonies. We were the first, and youngest, official Wedding Crashers on record. (My aunt asked me how things went on one particular occasion, and my reply was "Really good, but the bride was in a box." Following that cheerless ceremony, a yummy buffet lunch was served by church ladies, who happen to make the best quartered sandwiches on earth.) Now, to give you an example which nicely highlights my parenting skills, years after my kids had grown, a neighbour recounted, with long-lingering amusement, how my eyes stayed glued on them as they rode their bikes. I'll grudgingly admit that perhaps she had a point since we lived on a cul-de-sac and they could only go in circles, but why the hell would I give a rat's ass if I appeared nutty as long as they were safe?

As for my world view – we're banking on survival while hanging by a thread. For instance, no one can convince me that solutions are coming soon enough to prevent or even postpone the doomsday scenarios caused by climate change. Doing my part to help the environment is a must, but while we common folk are sorting out how to make dental floss from biodegradable silk and convert old flip-flops into placemats, progress needed to combat the much larger problems threatening our survival crawls at a snail's pace. But hope springs eternal, so there's that. There must always be hope.

As for how I treat myself – anxieties over external factors out of my control were always exacerbated with illogical personal behaviour (which theoretically would be in my control). It was quite the paradox. I'd risk being tarnished, but not admitting to a dreadful smoking habit would be lying about the true nature of my identity. It's important for me to be honest, but there was hesitation documenting this particular shortcoming. In the eyes of my grandchildren who may someday read this, I'd prefer to be thought of as *always* wise, an interactive playmate as malleable as a ragdoll at a tea party, the maker of magical carrots and mashed potatoes, and a greedy moocher of kisses. My openness would at least prove that there's no possible way to die from embarrassment. There was a worry that writing so honestly might kill me – and yes, the irony of my sentiment wasn't lost. But as Oliver Wendell Holmes famously said, "Sin has many tools, but a lie is the handle which fits them all."

In light of my diagnoses, a critical underlying question begged to be answered: Why bother following a highly restrictive GF diet and other medically required behaviour modifications to keep me healthy when clearly my disposition was hellbent on self-destruction? It was painful to face the fact that my life's tapestry was being woven with unwanted filaments of deep inner conflict entwined with the thread.

I had always managed my guilty conscience, by playing mind games. When jolts of panic reminded me of mortal frailty, some cockamamie scenario was visualized, where any lost time would, in the end, be defensible. Why not smoke and save myself from the horror of seeing morons, lacking stewardship skills, destroy my loved ones' future? Or, who the hell knows if a bear with exceptionally good taste might feast upon me tomorrow? To be truthful, though, mastering an addiction game felt like pushing a boulder uphill, knowing at some point it would tumble backwards to flatten me.

Deep down, my desire was to persevere and overcome my shortcomings. This meant no longer ignoring a body that wasn't exactly running like a fine-tuned machine. And, it couldn't be denied, my bad habit was assisting in dealing the grim reaper the upper hand. The Old Italian adage, *Il tempo non aspetta niente* – or "Time waits for nothing" – was suddenly a frightfully real prospect. That said, I wondered if a strictly regimented lifestyle might only be possible if in a coma, or living as a monk squirrelled away in a monastery somewhere in the Himalayas.

My life had become the textbook definition of contradiction – on the one hand there was security, comfort, and gratefulness for experiencing that rare, indescribable love that swallows you whole, along with very healthy habits, and, some will say, admirable attributes; on the other, there was always that incessant, self-punishing jitterbug nonsense dancing about in my head.

They say that when you reach some magical "mature" moment, days seem to fly by faster, and, as angels are my witness, it seemed plausibly true. If the adage could prompt me to quickly reform, weighty matters of the conscience might consist of nothing other than pondering over why my once hairy legs rarely need shaving but my chin now needs constant plucking.

$\mathcal{V}.2$

*"Before you diagnose yourself with depression
or low esteem first make sure that you are not
in fact surrounding yourself with assholes."*

~Steven Winterburn

e all grow into our adult vessels one way or another, and it's a good thing that most bumps in the road usually smooth out on their own over time. Ongoing obstacles, however, like unchecked anxiety; a rickety crutch crafted from rolled tobacco leaves; or acceptance of a cosmic joke which permanently disallows a Virgo, whose sign relates to wheat, from partaking in the sharing of foods at communal dining tables splendidly dusted with breadcrumbs, were unresolved issues.

It was tempting to seek advice, but I'd skipped down that path before, having visited various therapists over the years – rarely returning after a few initial appointments. I knew it was a fruitless endeavour because I was too afraid to be open and honest. I'd hide my greatest fear – looking like a fruitcake – beneath a carefully cultivated persona that rivalled that of the Dalai Lama. In other words, I carried myself as though I held the wisdom of the ages. Though my performance was stellar, I had the sneaking suspicion that a good therapist would be able to spot a nut too tough to crack, while no doubt wondering why they'd bother dispensing advice to someone not willing to admit she needs it.

My final therapy session, years before the CD diagnosis, ended in spectacular fashion. The only thing missing was a piñata filled with nerve pills, given as my participation award. I'd found a new therapist who appeared to have the skills of a homing pigeon, and who quickly zeroed in on the two main reasons for my visit – chronic anxiety and smoking – assuring me hypnosis was the answer. "What the hell?" It wasn't like she was suggesting a lobotomy. Moreover, without unlocking the door to expose the mystery of suppressed triggers impacting my current behaviour, I might never overcome a damn thing.

Yet there I was on the lovely settee, snapping myself back to the present before anything further could be revealed – so terrified of the images unfolding you'd think by my reaction the Holy Ghost had poked me in the ass. If a traumatic event actually happened to me as a little girl, it will remain a mystery, because there'll be no more mind-bending hocus-pocus.

Instead of the therapist going on an archeological dig into the deepest recesses of my mind, I'd have preferred that, after helping me achieve an altered state, she'd simply used the power of suggestion to anchor in the fact that anxiety is unproductive and thinking smoking relieves it is nothing more than a convenient myth.

Truth be told, full exposure of the memory wouldn't have evoked warm and fuzzy feelings, because it involved the bedroom located in the duplex above ours, where Mrs. L., the widowed owner of the property, resided. Someone with little imagination had sanctioned the use of utilitarian dark gray paint in the basement laundry room and carried it up the walls of the adjoining hallway and into this upper bedroom, making it feel like an extension of the spooky underbelly of the house and a perfect spot for ghosts to congregate. It's too bad no one bothered to consult the know-it-all little kid living downstairs, because I would've deemed the décor choice dreadful and vetoed it immediately.

The room was sparsely furnished, with not much other than a black rotary phone sitting on a small nightstand beside the bed. As kids, we were always welcome to freely roam upstairs, but that cheerless room was avoided – at least most of the time if the image under hypnosis had validity. I'd much prefer remembering Mrs. L.'s delightfully cheery kitchen, especially on days when the block of freshly made firm cottage cheese was delivered, which she'd open with care before serving me a chunky piece.

Memories aside, be they faded or obscured by design, there's only a few tangible items from my past that can be found in the basement; but there's a link, nonetheless, and it cannot be ignored. Life isn't lived in separate acts, so there's bound to be some type of invisible baggage carried forward. Speaking of baggage reminds me of my mother's two-joke repertoire. Neither of the jokes could tickle a funny bone, but we'd chuckle at the absurdity. One was about a guy at the hardware store purchasing wood to build a thirty-foot-long box to mail a clothesline; the other was about a conductor on a train repeatedly warning a passenger to move his baggage out of the aisle or he'd toss it off the train. After repeated warnings the conductor finally made good on his threat, and then turned to the passenger and said, "See, I told you I'd do it, and I did it. What do you think about that, sir?" The passenger replied, "Not much. It wasn't mine." Unfortunately, tossing personal baggage out a window was never an option, though the thought was certainly appealing.

Shy and sensible, nary a soul would catch me dancing nude in the rain trying to conjure up long-lost spirits. Soul-searching through hypnosis seemed just as ridiculous a ritual, but perhaps there's a reason yet to be unearthed that might go to the heart of why I've always referred to myself as "a wee tad bit of a wreck."

Damning the rain as it washed away perfectly executed chalk art off the sidewalk didn't contribute to the onset of anxiety, but there's one notable occasion among a few to choose from that might sensibly be considered a major trigger. When I was no bigger than knee-high to a grasshopper, Mother hauled me off to see a young doctor who was a temporary fill-in at the office we attended. His oversized frame had no doubt worn out the ratty Birkenstock-looking sandals he padded in on, and his long hair and beard were gnarly enough to easily hide a pair of hummingbirds. A rumpled flannel shirt completed the nerdy-groovy look. Let's just say he needed more than a little sprucing up.

He pulled out a piece of thread from God knows where, first holding it taut between his fingers then quickly jerking it until it broke into two pieces. "Colette, this is how fragile life is, and it takes a split second for it to end." For added effect he paused for a surreal moment of silence as I sat there, stunned. If ever a kid deserved a treat after a doctor's appointment, this confrontation certainly qualified, and, make no bones about it, it was going to take a lot more than a precious hotdog to appease me in my rattled state.

Was this hippy-dippy and possibly psychedelically enlightened doctor telling me the truth, or was he lying? In my opinion, both. The strongest, healthiest man on earth has no power to stop a catastrophic cardiac event and will surely die, and a sickly infant who seems fated to die can defy the odds and miraculously survive. How to accept the statement depended solely on my interpretation of "fragile," but being far too young to rationalize, I left the office gripped in terror, certain the revelation offered was both true and literal. Good God, we'd attended for an assessment following a lousy fender bender, and you'd think we'd survived the sinking of the Titanic.

To put it bluntly, the good doctor was an asshole, and a self-righteous one at that, more suited to squatting on a busy sidewalk somewhere, with a spliff in one hand and a cardboard sign with Jesus' name scrawled on it in the other. In the blink of an eye his thread analogy tethered to me like a flapping kite in a wind gust, with the potential to cause unsteady missteps on my journey into adulthood. If he was planning to further specialize in, God forbid, psychiatry, let me assure you he had yet to start the course.

Though not carefree by nature, I was, like any child, an innocent when we walked into his office. The doctor's revelation immediately entrenched itself into my psyche, which explains why, when we walked out of his office, the road appeared to have widened in the short time since we'd crossed it on arrival, and how stupidly reckless of Mother to contemplate crossing it again. Come to think of it, if we were going to risk life and limb to cross the street, at the very least, there bloody well should've been a hotdog stand on the other side, because eating a hotdog is usually a pretty good idea under any circumstance.

Apart from this new hyper-awareness of life's fragility, in contradictory fashion, fate had no doubt dealt me a good hand – there were no bootstraps to pull up and no need to become a stowaway in a seedy boxcar. That said, my plate was still pretty full, dealing with things like the ghostly apparitions that I instinctively knew had now found their way into the walk-in closet next to my bed; the dread of a neighbourhood nonna casting a mystery spell after her grand-children warned me that she had an Evil Eye; or Mother's threatening mantras that would result in disciplinary measures that stung like hell if not adhered to. A slipper might warm the foot but it doesn't warm the heart when it's weaponized. Now there was yet another thing, this snapping thread theory, to fret over.

Indeed, thanks to a variety of influences, including that of the good doctor, a disproportionate amount of my existence had been spent under a cloud of impending doom. Yet, oddly enough, when it suited me, I'd breech safe parameters (referring to my smoking habit) and tempt an unpleasant fate. Many of us tempt it by taking some sort of risk, after weighing the potential consequences against gratification, but it's all relative. A high-wire tightrope walker can strut his feathers all he wants, but his gratification comes from accomplishing nothing other than the panicky chicken with feathers flying, who saves himself from a KFC bucket by managing to cross the street, for no good reason other than getting to the other side.

The messengers, many with shaky credentials at best, were delivering warnings that were never requested and certainly not appreciated. And, to this day, trying to determine how their respective roles impacted my worldview is as befuddling as figuring out what came first, the chicken or the egg. With so many sources of information available, it boils down to either being baffled by bullshit or dazzled by brilliance.

$\mathcal{V}.3$

ithout a revelation from the hypnotherapy session I abruptly ended, any personal challenges were never seriously contemplated to be related to thread, ghosts, evil spells or quirky mantras from a bygone era. However, since most issues were now food-related, I wondered how far a gloriously gluten-laden ball of dough could be rolled out – it turns out, it would be all the way back to that Toronto neighbourhood of my childhood.

With no capacity to skip back in time for verification and no optical wizardry to allow me another peek at long-ago events, my only reliable resource was that somewhat stocky little girl I'd once been, and who still lived within, to sort things out, sum things up, and report back.

In the '60s, the area surrounding the bustling intersection of St. Clair Ave and Dufferin St was predominately comprised of hardworking Italians, most with large broods of bambinos, and a few remaining elderly Jewish people. Toss in my French-Canadian mother and Irish-Canadian father, and you get the picture.

Our duplex on the corner of Northcliffe Boulevard and Cloverlawn Ave was situated on one end of the block and St. Clare's Catholic Church and School were located on the other. As appearances were of paramount importance to Mother, one could safely assume that the prominent corner-to-corner position with the Godly institutions gave her some sort of moral superiority.

The occasions when Father Polito dined with us, for example, were sacred events for which she meticulously prepared. Most of her considerable efforts were focused not on the meal but on the appearance of piety: the ironed black-checkered dress, neatly coiffed bonnet of jet-black hair, flaming red lipstick, black butterfly glasses polished and sparkly; presentation of her children as angels; her house and yard, impeccable; and her affable but stubbornly laid back, chain-smoking, beer-drinking, non-practicing Protestant husband dressed neatly in a white shirt and ordered to behave with the appropriate reverence. Though Dad complied with the dress code, I've no doubt that he struggled to stop himself from trying to tickle the funny bone of a priest decked out in Holy garb. As for Mother, once her vision of perfection was accomplished and we were properly assembled on the front porch, she'd beam with pride, nervously awaiting his grand arrival. And, if by chance the God-fearing *Signora* next door happened to catch a glimpse of the blessed spectacle, her prayers were surely answered. It was, always, all about the optics.

When it came to the internal workings of our house, it was pretty apparent my parents didn't share equal billing on the marquee. Mother wrote the script, directed the show, and had the starring role. For the most part, she was harmless – sometimes funny, proud and prudish, reclusive unless in the company of others, and bitingly critical.

She ran an efficient household, the result of having been properly trained in all things domestic. This training included knitting and sewing, and it shames me to admit my sister Denise and I had little patience for it. We were never as thrilled as she was with one of her latest creations, but instead merely tolerated the long, drawn-out process of standing while patterns were repeatedly altered. Her thread, one could assume, was a little more durable than that of the asshole doctor.

Of course, there were a few smashing successes, including the stylish vinyl baby-blue capes that were all the rage. My personal favourite, though, was Mother's first project – a fabulous reproduction of the classic white nurse's uniform. After each sewing project was completed, she'd twirl us in front of the armoire mirror, proudly proclaiming that we were the luckiest of poor-little-rich-girls. She repeated the mantra (as she interpreted its meaning) often, as a reminder that being rich had nothing to do with our meagre finances, but instead, the luxury of decent circumstances. And she was right.

Denise and I were excellent stewards of our make-believe hospital but would soon outgrow our uniforms and lose the plastic syringes and doodads for checking reflexes that came with our little black medical bags. As we transitioned from make-believe to explore the world beyond the boundaries of the living room, Mother too, transitioned. Happening subtly, with no obvious event to explain it, there'd be limited interaction with us once the perfunctory tasks of dousing us with talcum powder after our bath or teaching us to pray in French had run their course.

"Mother's First Sewing Project" Colette and Denise mid '60's

I've often wondered whether the circumstances of my birth had somehow damaged the nurturing process. Mother was thirty-five years old (thirteen years younger than Dad), when I arrived by C-section – this, after months of hospitalization due to complications during the pregnancy. One of the issues, ironically, was a condition where the Rh blood factor of mother and baby is not a match. I'm sure technology has evolved, but at the time, it was critical that immediately following delivery, the "blue baby" undergo an immediate blood transfusion if there were any hope for survival. Considering that she'd already endured more than her share of suffering, namely thirteen months in an iron lung contraption in a sanatorium during her lengthy battle with tuberculosis, the unpleasant experience of birthing her second child may have left an indelible mark.

This is going a bit off track, but, since breastmilk is early sustenance and my main theme is food-related, I'm going to go there. Denise, with no sane reason offered for the inquiry, wanted to know if we were breastfed. She would've been more productive seeking the answer from someone other than me (being the last one born), but my chirpy response was "Mother could've fed us Dad's warm beer using a turkey baster, and we'd be none the wiser." For most people, it's probably an utterly useless matter to bother contemplating, but it's something I was curious about, for all of a minute, considering Mother's laissez-faire attitude, in particular, towards me – along with wondering if the blood they transfused me with was donated by an Italian signora (which is meaningless too, of course, but a pleasant thought).

The mother-daughter bond may have been dangling by a loose thread from start to finish, but I'm grateful she didn't forgo having a second child, opting instead to buy Denise a porcelain baby doll to play with. We'd hear whispers of the hardships she endured by surviving a childhood with an authoritarian father and her grueling five-year odyssey with illness, so we instinctively knew she didn't mean to neglect our emotional needs, and we always showed respect. There's never been a need to over-analyze the situation, and it's healthier to laugh instead of cry, when chronicling past events or her quirky eccentricities. To be sure, she was strong in will, but perhaps quite tired in spirit. And she was loved.

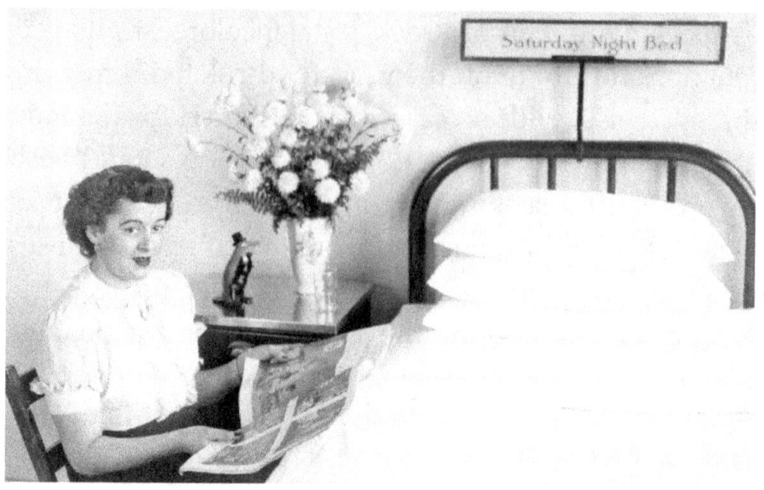

"Mother at the Muskoka Sanitorium" circa 1945
Jeanne Francis (Bertrand) Sullivan

I'm adding a note here, after just finding an album belonging to Mother that was never examined. Somewhere, sandwiched between her childhood, her illness and her marriage, there was an independent career woman, as seen in snippets of prestige employment announcements. The pictures revealed a vivacious woman who exuded grace. A woman so impeccably dressed one could conjure up the image of her sharing a walk-in closet with Jacqueline Kennedy Onassis. This woman, a stranger, is someone my own eyes didn't see. I don't know how she calculated wins and losses, and on what side of the scoreboard motherhood experiences landed on. But I do know that they say a picture can paint a thousand words – they can also write a good mystery book.

The ensuing result of her disinterest protected us from pratfalls, those unforgettable lessons kids learn by being personally engaged with parents who are teaching them, even at the cost of being bruised and hurt.

It's not that things were bad, but interactions with Mother were strictly limited to the mundane, everyday matters at hand. The cat we'd never own sure as hell didn't bite her tongue, but in our house, they're be no intimate motherly fireside chats. The feminist movement was under-way and women were daring to start an honest dialogue about where they'd *really* like to shove the poultry dressing, but nothing prodded her into helping us find deeper, more meaningful connections to the world, beyond her own, personal scope, which was obviously narrowing with time.

If she deemed our future roles would be domesticated housewives, at the very least she could've pretended that aprons arrive with the placenta of a female child (odd, but the notion quite pleases me – an apron is known as a front-facing superhero's cape worn around the waist). We were completely oblivious to the notion that childhood is a springboard for catapulting you into the adult world of work and responsibility, and without this knowledge there was no need to dream of how we might like to position ourselves once there. The only sensible path forward, I'd soon determine at a tender age, was to grow up and become an Italian who could cook, thus, learning the universal language of love as it relates to broken bread, pasta and sauce. Not to be harsh, but the simple adage she could've afforded her daughters would simply have stated: "Be ladies in the parlour, chefs in the kitchen, and acrobats in the bedroom." She managed to continue our upkeep, making sure we were well-dressed and well-mannered, perhaps hoping that this would be enough to eventually produce well-rounded women.

～

With her efficiency at running the household, and because she was only away from home occasionally to fill in as a teacher, Mother had ample time and wherewithal to hone the dying art of how to "Dine on a Dime & on Time." Her no-nonsense practicality ensured her success. Another favourite mantra from her repertoire of one-liners was the powdered milk chant, used to indoctrinate me into believing it was much tastier than real milk. The large plastic bag was filled with pebbly yellow granules, and, when opened, had an odour even a horse would turn its nose up at – neigh, neigh!

Mother was enlisted with maintaining the property, as well as tending to the personal needs of the widowed Mrs. L upstairs. While Mrs. L had a spare bedroom, which, as mentioned, was as drab as a dungeon, her dining room was on par with her kitchen, which was nothing short of dreamy. The large ornate sideboard had this spectacular candelabrum along with intricately etched silver antiquities for all manner of serving, carefully set out on doilies. The high-back chairs were majestically positioned around an ebony lacquered dining room table, beckoning to be of service to esteemed company schooled in the art of appreciating the finer things in life. It was just about as perfect a sight as I'd ever seen.

Our dining room, on the other hand, became a casualty of Mother's practicality (at least as she defined the word), when she converted this room with the gleaming hardwood floors into a bedroom for Dad. Her own sleeping quarter was a room we rarely entered – my most memorable recollection of it was on the day JFK died, when she sat on her bed in stone-cold silence watching the horror unfold, oblivious to anyone's presence. After the conversion was made, company entering the house from the front door had to make their way through the living room and Dad's newly-fashioned bedroom in order to congregate in the kitchen. It ensured that hosting any type of formal dining was permanently set aside. There was no sense in it, which was proven to me without doubt, when shortly thereafter, Aunt Hazel, logically thinking of her own layout, converted her spare bedroom into a dining room.

Now mind you, Mother still managed to entertain, even without the frivolous trappings of a dining room. On special occasions like Christmas, which were more costly and time-consuming affairs to assemble, she'd pull us aside before the festivities began to remind us, as usual (I'd say ad nauseam), that we were the luckiest of poor-little-rich-girls and under no circumstance were we to touch the exorbitantly expensive butter set out for the company. Denise and I would nod obediently, though truthfully, we couldn't have cared less about the butter, so delirious with the joy we felt at having so many wonderful things to eat and guests to share them with.

It was a dicey decision at best when Denise suggested we host a festive event to honour Mother, without prior approval or supervision. Denise was eight at the time, and I was six. In the wee morning hours of Mother's Day, we slipped from our beds and went to the kitchen, dragging chairs to the counter in order to prep the work area. Denise carefully went through a cookbook and had little need to convince me of her selection. We happily agreed upon the only truly impressive option available, and production of the "Wedding Cake" was underway.

Injuries inflicted that day were limited to Denise's ego. Of course, there'd be no physical repercussions because, as the golden child, she had my parents wrapped around her dainty fingers and could easily get away with anything. She was the beautifully flowering tendril, with shimmering blond hair, full pink pouty lips, doe-like brown eyes, and to top things off, a beauty mole perfectly positioned on the left side of her peaches-and-cream cheeks. Our older half-sister Lynn (Dad's daughter with his first wife), resembled Denise and was also wisp-like, fair, and freckled, with beautiful long locks of strawberry hair. I, of sturdier, heartier French stock, with ordinary brown hair, was saddled with the moniker "Bull-In-A-China-Shop." My preference for a nickname, however, was "Curly," as Mrs. L., fondly, called me.

Our foray into the world of upscale baking had come to an abrupt halt, and Denise's dream of the kudos that would surely follow the presentation of such an inspired work of art now lay broken, much like the dozen eggs swimming about with bits of broken shell in mounds of sugary flour. Mother was far from pleased, to say the least, shooing us off as she attempted to salvage what she could of the Wedding Cake. Whether or not she succeeded is a mystery, because I've no recollection of eating a piece.

It was unsettling that adults didn't appear to be fond of their daily grind, because a glumness surrounded their routines. Mother, in particular, wearing her zippered housedress that resembled a uniform, could be found each morning sitting at the end of the kitchen table with a coffee and smoke, expressionless. It's notable though, that the parade of teen-aged girls, relatives or family acquaintances, staying with us temporarily for varying reasons, seemed to be immune from misery, and, as I wasn't yet part of this elite group, you can rely on my unvarnished account of their blessed auras as they happily primped and preened before a Saturday night out. Sumptuous spa-like housecoats with fluffy slippers were the requisite attire before donning miniskirts, which were laid out on the utilitarian, second-hand bedspread. Back then they could iron their outfits, iron their hair, and quickly iron themselves the perfect grilled cheese sandwich. For the grand finale, they'd spray their beehives into a tizzy. Whenever they were present in the house, it buzzed with their groovy energy, so much so, the curtains, lamps and doilies seemed to swing right along with Petula Clark as she belted out her gorgeous tune, "Downtown." Jealousy of the older girls was never harboured on my part, but there was a realization that Elvis and his ilk didn't have a stocky kid like me in mind when crooning the kitschy tunes that defined the era.

According to family folklore, in the early formative years Mother would harness me whenever I was outdoors. There was never a reason for me to have an issue with this because she secured my safety, but I marvel at the absurdity. When my unleashing came, concurrent with her detachment, it set me as free as a bird. I've never doubted for a moment that this freedom was crucial to my happiness as a child, and for one simple reason: it led me to beautiful, authentic neighbourhood Italian food. *"Hearken diligently unto me, and eat ye that which is good, and let your soul delight itself in fatness."* <u>Isaiah 55:2</u> (KJV) [i]

V.4

"We do not remember days, we remember moments. The richness of life lies in memories we have forgotten.

~Pavese Cesare

Our kitchen, like most, was the gathering spot in our home. Dad would sit in a sleeveless white undershirt, often strumming his banjo, chain-smoking, a warm Molson Stock Ale in hand; and Mother, in her housedress, would be mixing rice and raisins for rice pudding, our standard dessert. For me, rice pudding wasn't a treat. It's as asinine as attempting to whip up something festive by frying roasted beer nuts with eggs and proclaiming the ridiculous creation of "Nutty Egg Nougat." I'm not ungrateful and realize that rice is an essential staple prized for its medicinal purposes among other things, but according to my personal food log from childhood, things like rice and raisins should be rendered asunder. If I'd been diagnosed with CD in childhood, as a matter of convenience, Mother probably would've made a year's supply of rice pudding as a way to sustain me.

Only cold comfort could be found with other staples she insisted on, like liver and onions, or mincemeat tarts at Christmas. I only have to hear mention of a "Nanaimo Bar" and my stomach does an ungraceful backflip. She may have been uninspired culinary wise, but her scrambled eggs, Yorkshire pudding, and gravies would've been considered award-worthy.

Dad wasn't interested in kitchen matters, the exception being Friday nights, when he made his chili. While watching Saturday night sitcoms like *The Patty Duke Show* and *The Flying Nun*, we'd have the chili along with homemade French fries for dipping, as Mother had mastered the art of using a deep fryer. She used Tenderflake lard and, mother of pearl, the fries were good. The following morning, after church, we'd go to Sherman's Bakery to pick up bagels, and the days-old chili, now thicker and richer, would be spooned on top, resulting in perfectly mingled chili-butter. Swirling and spilling over the sides from the heat, it needed to be licked up quickly to avoid dripping on our Sunday best.

The pot of chili magically attracted company, which seemed to please my dad, but sometimes when alone, this gentle soul wore his discontent on his sleeve. During rainstorms he would sit on the front porch, staring out as if entranced while flicking cigarettes over the banister onto the lawn. I remember being freshly bathed, clad in pajamas and exhausted, frantically pleading for him to come in to safety, for both our sakes. My pleas fell on deaf ears. Apparently, he adored the chaos of thunder and lightning. A storm usually provoked his lamentation of how sick and tired he was of the "damn rat race," which referred to his definition of city-life, and perhaps life in general.

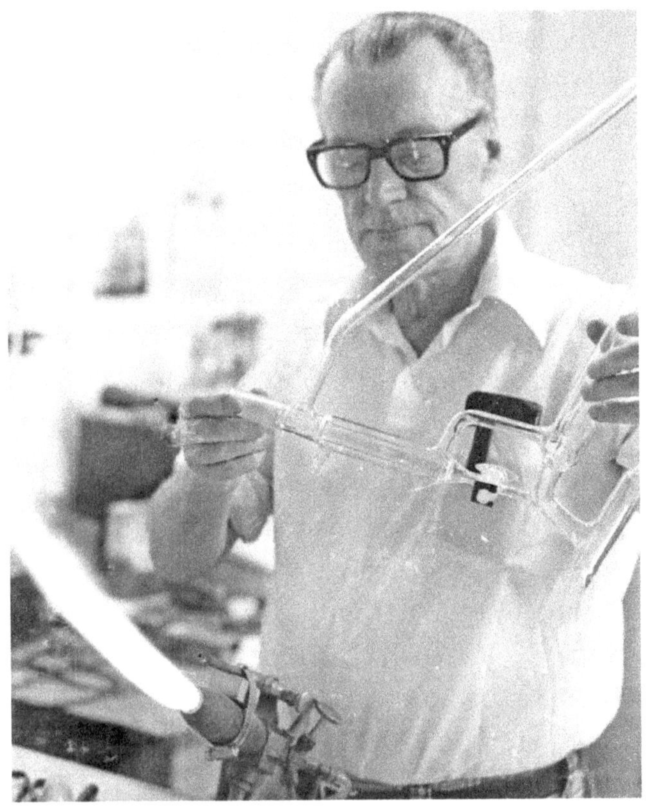

"Dad in his North Bay Glass Shop" circa mid '70s – John Henry Sullivan

I'm adding a note here too, after examining more of the treasure trove of snippets found in Mother's album. I came across a newspaper article where Dad explains he began his full-time career, at thirteen years of age, blowing glass casings for radio tubes at the Northern Electric Co. of Montreal. He traveled with a caravan blowing glass ornaments, worked at the Atomic Research Council of Canada, and worked with many scientific glass blowing shops throughout North America. I don't know how he calculated wins and losses, or who, what, when, where, or why led to his "damn rat race" sentiment. But one could imagine the stark contrasts in his life, from travelling-caravan freedom to a dependable middle-aged man with ankle-biters to raise.

As part of a dying breed of scientific glassblowers, in his time, Dad was considered one of the best in the world. This highly-skilled trade paid no dividends for dedication and talent but at least afforded him a Dodge to drive to work. Evenings were spent working in his basement glass shop, where he'd blow all sorts of intricate glassware for laboratories and would gladly blow a swan, elephant, or hash pipe if asked. He often expressed regret that his day job designing and producing neon signs didn't come close to utilizing his scientific expertise.

I was too young to appreciate his skill and artful talent, but I'll never forget the sight of him, carefully transporting our dying pet goldfish down to the asbestos workbench, patiently trying to revive it with oxygen. On a personal note, it was painful to learn our goldfish wouldn't survive my dish-soap-bubble-bath beauty regimen. As for my well-intention-ed but over-the-top pet care, I'd come up with novel ideas on a per-project basis, which is why there's no explanation as to how the newts, which replaced the goldfish, both managed to lose their tails on the same day.

I cannot remember what plate of pasta sealed the deal to make Italian food a crucial distraction, but another pet would also have kept my mind occupied – as long as it had the potential to live longer than a week. Denise had found us a turtle to buy, but she knew Mother would never agree to it. She decided we'd buy it anyways, reasoning that, if we named it Francis in honour of her middle name, she'd be thrilled with the new addition to the family. She wasn't.

Dad tried to help us win Mother's approval. He built Francis a fancy little house decked out with all she'd need to be happily contained. But then he crossed a line by allowing the turtle a bit of freedom. Mother would watch in horror as it crawled along on the kitchen table. The experience of getting up close and personal was a lot of fun for us, but by her reaction you'd think she was standing bare-naked and exposed to danger in the middle of an African lion sanctuary.

Francis sat in her box on the rear window ledge of the car as we drove her to her new home at the lake where she was released. We sobbed uncontrollably during the entire ride. She'd come from a pet store, and it's fair to say she may have initially enjoyed her new, *natural* environment, but it probably wasn't entertaining for long. If there was a silver lining, it was that there was no attempt to make turtle soup.

After the failed attempt at saving my pet goldfish, the replacement newts' demise shortly thereafter, and the heartbreaking turtle loss, I pined for a dog, but Mother was far too practical to entertain the idea of getting one. In fairness to her, it might've been a dream seeing how she abruptly made the lost, somewhat scruffy-looking poodle at the door disappear. So, one can only imagine my sheer delight when arriving at the Italian market on St. Clair to find my new pets – yes, two pets – and well within my limited budget. There before me were bushels of beautiful snails, creatures so small in size Mother wouldn't even notice their existence. Being at nose and eye level with such a large array was a little offensive, but still a sight to behold. Hellbent on giving them a home, I was off to find a jar. Upon my return to search out the perfect pair, the grocer, with large scoop in hand, was shoveling what had to be hundreds into a bag for Signora. It didn't go unnoticed that the kids in her house were getting a bag full, but my purchase pleased me just the same. Thankfully, Signora never waved me in when their pets were swimming in sizzling broth.

If snails didn't belong in a pot, neither did fish. The offensive smell had been endured often enough, and the built-up courage needed to investigate the source finally arrived. In Mrs. L's kitchen upstairs, the simmering pot sat on the stove, and once a chair was dragged over and lid removed, the main ingredient looked back at me. If I never again see a bright-eyed fish, with slivers of onion like bait to its mouth, bobbing along in simmering broth, it'll still be too soon. Cousin Maureen tells me she thinks gefilte fish was being prepared for Passover and says it's delicious. I'll gladly take her word.

It was the little things Dad did that tickled us, like how he managed our disappointment on days when Mother was serving the dreaded liver dinner. Without his kindness, it's fair to say I might've run off with a travelling circus to avoid the repulsiveness of it all. But being the obedient-to-a-fault child that I was (my perception, not Mother's), I always somehow managed to choke it down. Denise would simply toss her liver behind the radiator.

After dinner, Dad congratulated us by tossing coins in the air, which we wisely spent on penny candy. Funny gesture, because there wasn't a snowball's chance in hell that Denise's indiscretion wouldn't be discovered, as Mother cleaned with the precision of a drill sergeant, and we didn't have a hungry stray poodle to devour the evidence. Golden child, to be sure!

Each evening I'd stand on a chair watching out the pantry window awaiting Dad's arrival, looking like my goldfish out of water, gasping for air, if he happened to be a few minutes late. His faithful return, it seemed to me, was because he wouldn't want to miss supper. Call it what you want, food was the bait needed for a good catch, and picturing him seated at the kitchen table, even on liver days, was proof that a decent meal worked wonders at reeling him in.

Resilient threads of wisdom got snagged in the very few conversations shared between us. Sadly, the words are long forgotten, but it doesn't change the fact that he was the glue that held my world together.

<u>Mother's Scrambled Eggs</u>

Initially, I couldn't imagine who in hell would want a recipe for scrambled eggs, of all things, but Mother's eggs were velvety, and there had to be a reason for what set them apart. Funny enough, it turns out there's a method to follow if you don't want hard little rubbery lumps. Some recipes call for the addition of cream or milk, and I suspect Mother used milk, but I get great results without adding either of them.

Ingredients

4 eggs, fresh free-range, whisked so they're light and airy

¾ tbsp butter

Pinch of salt

Directions

Use a whisk, instead of a fork, to blend the yolks and whites more evenly. Add a pinch of salt. Set stovetop to medium-low heat, or lower depending on your stove, so you can cook the eggs slowly. Melt the butter and add eggs to a small, heavy-bottomed enamelled saucepan or a good quality non-stick pan. Using a silicone spatula, begin gently nudging the edges of the mixture inward as it starts to form fluffy curds. If necessary, take the pan off the heat for a moment during the cooking process to avoid any chance of browning. When they're just about set, remove from heat. Serve immediately.

GF Yorkshire Pudding

Yorkshire pudding is an odd name, because the batter will bake into a bun, which looks a bit like puff pastry. The buns will be a beautiful golden color and a little crispy on the outside, yet dreamily tender and chewy on the inside.

Ingredients

⅔ cup (GF) flour

⅔ cup cornstarch or tapioca starch (may be sold as tapioca flour)

½ tsp salt

3 eggs

1 cup milk

Lard (You can also use oil, fat drippings from roast, or bacon fat)

Directions

Preheat oven to 425°F.

In a large mixing bowl, whisk together the flour, starch and salt until combined.

In a large measuring cup, whisk together the milk and eggs until thoroughly mixed.

Add the milk and egg mixture into the flour mixture and whisk until smooth and thin.

Put a dollop of lard (about a tsp) into each well of a twelve-well muffin tin. Place the greased muffin tin into the oven as it preheats. Your muffin tin and oil should be hot, and slightly smoking, before adding your batter.

Once the oven has fully heated, remove the hot muffin tin. The batter must sizzle when filling the wells. Pour a bit of batter into the first well, and if it isn't sizzling, return your pan to the oven for a few minutes. Fill the wells about 3/4 full. Note: you may end up with 10 Yorkshire puddings, rather than 12, depending on how you distribute the batter.

Place the tin back in the middle of the oven and let bake for 20-25 minutes. The batter will puff up so make sure the rack above won't get in the way.

Serve immediately and enjoy. Delicious with butter and gravy.

Dad's Chili

Dad never gave me his recipe for chili, but with a few ingredients you can't go wrong with my version. He'd make a six or eight beer chili, depending on how his Friday night ritual unfolded. I'm not condoning his method, but it's worth a mention. Although this recipe is basic, it's got great flavour.

Ingredients

2 lbs ground chuck

½ large onion, diced

2 stalks celery, diced

⅓ green pepper, diced

⅓ red pepper, diced

2 garlic cloves, minced

1 48-oz. can of tomato juice

2 cans of red kidney beans, not rinsed

1½ tbsp brown sugar, more or less, to taste

2½ tbsp vinegar, more or less, to taste

3 tsp chili powder, more or less, to taste

½ tsp salt

1 tsp crushed red chili pepper, more or less, to taste

Cracked pepper

Directions

In a large pot, sauté meat with onions, celery, chopped peppers and garlic. Do not stir the meat aggressively to avoid further mincing it, while leaving some pieces a little larger than others. Once the meat is cooked, tilt the pot and spoon out the excess fat. Add the tomato juice, kidney beans and seasoning. Season with cracked pepper. Once the chili comes to a simmer you can adjust the seasonings if desired, as I've been quite conservative in my measurements.

Browned Flour for Gravy

Mother always browned her flour, and I suspect that's why her gravy was noteworthy. Heat a dry cast iron pan on medium-low. When the pan is hot enough, spread as much (GF) all-purpose white flour as needed to cover the bottom.

Stir the flour often with a wooden spoon or silicone spatula, keeping a very close eye on it once it starts to brown so it doesn't get too dark.

"A home cook who relies too much on a recipe is sort of like a pilot who reads the plane's instruction manual while flying."

~Alton Brown

To be honest, I wasn't entirely sure that adding a small selection of recipes to my story would be appropriate. Food is my thing, but I'm not a trained cook, and the definition of a "recipe", in my mind, is the gathering of simple ingredients to make a simple meal. If I were asked to appear on the Food Network, I'd look no more qualified than the Swedish Chef on the Muppets, donning a *toque blanche* (white hat), waving utensils around, and spewing gibberish. No doubt, due to some unfortunate mishap, by the start of the first commercial break my toque blanche wouldn't be needed, as I'd be *tout fini* (all done!).

Many of the everyday GF recipes I've chosen require flour, or breading, and are never a menu option when dining out, so I soothe my psyche by making them often at home. Sure, I have to do the prep, the cooking, and the clean-up, but the upside is that no craving goes unanswered. All of the recipes can be made using gluten-containing ingredients (only a few are specifically dedicated GF, and can't be converted).

I was off to a questionable start with Mother's nonexistent recipe for scrambled eggs, but I can assure you that I've recreated all the recipes using a proper weight scale and measuring spoons. My usual method is simply a "pinch of this and that," but I wanted to make sure that you'd get good results.

You will note in the recipes that follow a reference to a "Dutch Oven". This is simply a heavy-bottomed, thick-walled pot, with a heavy lid that fits snugly (mine are cast iron), which can be used on the stovetop or in the oven. Of course, as long as you're enjoying the process of cooking and a different type of vessel works, it's all good. It's my preference to use cast iron cookware whenever feasible, because they hold heat evenly, are chemical free, are naturally non-stick, and add iron to your food. My stovetop cooking unit is gas, with an open-flame, so you may have to adjust your cooking temperatures according to your type of stove.

The following list highlights my go-to kitchen staples, all naturally GF, along with tidbits of useful information. Missing from the list is garlic (see note in Glossary), just as cherished, good for warding off vampires, and always on hand. Please note that the information is accurate but rudimentary – for general interest only.

⌒

My Kitchen Staples

Sea Salt

You certainly don't need to use salt at all if you're consuming any type of processed food, because you're getting enough of it, but some foods are impossible to salvage from blandness if salt isn't used during the cooking process.

If you're wondering about any benefit to using "all natural" sea salt, the following excerpt from the American Heart Association will clear up any confusion:

"Sea salt has boomed in popularity in restaurants and super-market aisles across the country. Many gourmet chefs say they prefer it to table salt for its coarse, crunchy texture and stronger flavor. Manufacturers are using it in potato chips and other snacks because it's 'all natural,' and not processed like table salt. And some health-conscious consumers choose it because it contains minerals like magnesium."

"…Each of the above-mentioned characteristics may set sea salt apart from table salt, but in one other very important respect there's absolutely no difference between the two: sodium content." [ii]

Olive Oil

A good quality olive oil will have a seal to confirm its authenticity. Its flavour will have the fruitiness of fresh or un-ripened fruit, or green tomatoes, or will have a peppery bitterness. It will be full-

flavoured and aromatic. To maintain the freshness and the superior qualities that make olive oil so special, buy the oil in dark bottles instead of clear glass. Minimizing exposure to light will help it to stay fresh longer. Check best-before dates to ensure you're using it when it's at its peak potential.

The best olive oil is listed as "Extra Virgin." I use this type for any dish where the oil isn't heated, unless I'm sautéing on low heat.

Refined olive oil, "pure" or "olive pomace" is what you'll find in the large metal cans carried by the grocery store. It would be considered inferior in quality, and best to be used for higher temperature cooking, roasting or grilling.

"Extra Light" is the one to try if you prefer a less intense olive oil. Remember, the term only pertains to its lightness in flavour, not its caloric content.

Ghee

Ghee has been used for thousands of years in Indian and Pakistani cultures. It's similar to clarified butter, but due to a longer cooking process it has a nuttier flavour. In basic terms, the butter goes through a heating process which separates the milk solids and evaporates the liquids. The oil that remains is ghee. Unlike clarified butter, it's a product that's readily available in most grocery stores. Since it has a high smoking point, I prefer using it as a replacement when butter, rather than oil, would work better. Regular butter would smoke like flames from hell under intense heat. Ghee works exceptionally well when using a cast iron skillet. I'll set a dry skillet on high heat for several minutes before adding the ghee, followed by the meat. For steak: When the meat is cooked to rare, I'll turn down the heat and add a good dollop of fresh butter and a few thyme sprigs, tilting the pan so I can easily spoon the butter and herb over the meat several times. Once the steak is removed from the pan, I will let it rest for a few moments. It's a perfect medium-rare when plated.

Balsamic Vinegar

There's a great article written by Gayle A. Alleman titled, "Ultimate Guide to Vinegar," which I recommend googling if you're interested in reading about various vinegars. [iii]

Gayle explains that balsamic vinegar is not considered a wine product, because the grape pressings haven't been allowed to ferment into wine. Basically, the two types of balsamic vinegar are "traditional" or "commercial." The best of the traditional balsamic vinegars hail from Modena, in the northern part of Italy and are carefully crafted using traditional time-honoured methods of preparation. The average aging time is anywhere between six and twenty-five years.

Authentic vinegar from the Modena region is distinguished by a seal that states it belongs to the "Consortium of Producers of the Traditional Balsamic Vinegar of Modena." The bottle should have a Protected Designation of Origin (PDO), or Protected Geographical Indication label, (PGI – IGP in Italian).

Commercial vinegars may also hail from the Modena region. However, if balsamic vinegar does not carry a seal, the producers are not bound to follow set rules regarding method of preparation or aging process. The difference in taste between cheap commercial balsamic vinegar and one that's authenticated is noteworthy. Once you've had the good stuff, there's no going back.

Tomatoes

We were driving through farm country and stopped to purchase organic, grain-fed chicken, and, as we were leaving the rustic little shop, the owner told me to take as many heirloom tomatoes as I'd like out of the bushel on the floor. Since she was happy to give me the tomatoes free, a few were tucked into my bag, with thanks.

When we got into the car, I mentioned to Claude that I'd never seen tomatoes that looked so deformed and wondered whether they'd been ravaged by early frost or some other ailment. Every tomato was different in color – dark green, pale green, pink to red, and streaks of white. The skins were thick and rubbery, and the shapes looked alien. Let's just say that looks can be deceiving.

Once home, we sliced a few to taste and couldn't believe how absolutely delicious they were. I was sorry we didn't take the whole bushel.

As for my pasta sauce, San Marzano tomatoes from Italy are an absolute must. The tomato is grown in rich volcanic soil and resembles a plum tomato, but it's thinner, more pointed, has thicker flesh, fewer seeds, stronger taste, and is sweeter and less acidic.

There are many tomatoes masquerading as authentic San Marzano, which means you may be paying a pretty penny for a cheap knock-off. Look for the seals of certification, for example, "Pomodoro San Marzano dell'Agro Sarnese Nocerino D.O.P.", which may also have a certification number.

Unless local or grown from your own garden, tomatoes are usually picked before vine ripening to allow time for travel and cannot compare to a beautiful Italian vine-ripened tomato packed at its peak.

Wine

Many, many moons ago, back in our younger days, Claude and I were out for a rare, more upscale dinner than what was usual, and I was nervous as hell when he was handed the Wine List. We weren't exactly connoisseurs and might look foolish when ordering – you know, by asking if they might have an updated blend of Baby Duck on hand, which back in the day most teenagers drank by the boatload because it was a decently sweet buzz. Claude perused the list looking quite calm and suave, and opted for a foreign bottle of something unfamiliar. The waiter appeared with the bottle and cork-screw, popped the cork, and set it on the table, which just happened to be situated smack dab in the middle of the packed restaurant. Claude, matter-of-factly, picked up the cork and began sniffing it. I looked on, absolutely mortified, wondering if perhaps he did so due to nervous reflex, or instinctively knew of this shmaltzy ritual from a prior life. As far as I was concerned, he may as well have asked the waiter to lift his arm so he could sniff his armpit. As it turns out, it was an impressive manoeuvre for a rookie wine drinker, but I still cringe when thinking back to my reaction. Of course, you should sniff the cork for any hint of mould!

Unfortunately, I'm still on the lower end of the scale when it comes to wine culture knowledge, but I do like to get things right when serving wine with dinner. I also make certain to follow the golden rule – never cook with a wine you wouldn't drink.

Listed below are a few simple suggestions for serving wine, which, of course, could be either expanded upon or perhaps disputed, depending on personal preference. The information obtained was found at Food & Wine.com.

Use Chardonnay for fatty fish or rich sauce; Champagne for anything salty; Cabernet Sauvignon with juicy red meat; Sauvignon Blanc with tart dressings and sauces; Dry Rosé for rich cheesy entrees; Pinot Grigio with light fish dishes; Malbec with sweet-spicy barbeque sauces; Syrah with highly spiced dishes; Zinfandel with pates, mousses and terrines; Off-Dry Riesling with sweet and spicy dishes; Rosé Champagne with main courses and hors d'oeuvres; and Old World Wines with old world dishes where the wine grapes and the food have grown in the same area for centuries.

Herbs

Fresh herbs are wonderful, but until recently, I would've used cilantro only if performing an exorcism. It's slowly growing on me when eating Indian food, but I find it can overpower a dish. Dill is another herb that I'm not terribly fond of using in large quantity, although a sprinkle on salmon or a pinch used in a fish marinade is quite nice.

The fresher the herbs the merrier, and in my kitchen the essentials are usually basil and oregano with pasta and tomato dishes, thyme with soups, and rosemary and oregano with pork and chicken.

I use an abundance of basil, so once the temperature isn't dropping below freezing, I plant four to six small basil plants from the nursery in a big pot on my front deck, which has northern exposure so there's late-afternoon-to-evening sun. I keep the moisture level consistent and never over-water. The plants grow into one big bush, so perhaps the location and watering matters.

Parmesan Cheese

Excerpt from parmesan.com: "History of Parmesan Cheese."

"In 2008, European courts decreed that Parmigiano Reggiano is the only hard cheese that can be legally called Parmesan. In so doing, they acknowledge the historical fact that the word can be traced to Parma and that consumers associate the cheese with its origin in the Parma-Reggio region of Italy. These court rulings mean that a cheese cannot be called Parmesan unless it conforms to the Protected Designation of Origin (PDO) standards for Parmigiano Reggiano." [iv]

The crafting of this particular cheese requires expert rituals that date back nine centuries. It's expensive, but versatile and worth every cent. Should a small piece become too dry for grating I put it in a sealed bag in the freezer for use when making sauce. Toss the chunk in to enhance the flavour.

I use Parmigiano Reggiano for finishing off a dish or for applications where the excellent quality and flavour can be appreciated. Grated cheese in grocery stores simply labelled as "Parmesan" may not even be made in Italy, and will be inferior to Parmigiano Reggiano, so it's more suitable for use when making my Queijo buns (recipe in Vignette 5), mixing into breadcrumb mixtures, and adding to sauces.

Onions

I use a variety of onions when cooking, but I'm singling out Vidalia. First produced in low sulfur soil in Georgia in the early 1930s, they soon became prized as unusually sweet and unique. The Vidalia onion is the official State of Georgia vegetable, and both state and federal law strictly regulate the production area. I love these onions and buy them by the bagful, because come late fall they're gone and won't be back again until the next spring. Some people wait for the Easter Bunny, but I wait for the arrival of Vidalia onions.

V.5

"It was quite simple. Food was the unifier. And I was in the perfect position, height-wise, to intimately know this."

~ Colette

Dinnertime was the only occasion when we'd function in unison, all with fork in hand. Who knows, maybe there was a ringing bell only audible to adults, because it was a ritual the entire neighbourhood would partake in at precisely the same time each evening. In our house, though, there was little conversation once the mouth was full of food. Without food as a unifier, and the kitchen as the center of the universe, Mother could've hired a body double and traveled the seven seas and I'd have been hard-pressed to notice.

To be fair, there were instances of fond interaction with her. When she was making canned salmon sandwiches (an expensive and thus rare treat) for Dad's lunch the next day, the smell would wake me out of a dead sleep, and I remember her being patient by my appearance. Standing with my head just above the counter's height, I found the fish smell intense, and the look of the bones and skin were off-putting; however, unlike the fish found in Mrs. L's pot in the kitchen upstairs, I liked salmon and was more than excited for a taste test. Salmon made with lots of chopped dill pickle, thinly sliced onion, mayo, and topped off with a thick tomato slice is a classic favourite. When I'm eating a salmon sandwich now, I fondly think back to those rare, pleasant, one-on-one encounters with her.

Having lunch in a restaurant was never a stand-alone event, or a fanciful whim – there had to be a good reason to explain the outing, and Mother's need for a bra *always* seemed to top the list of explanations. There may not be a suitable word to describe her dogged determination when it came to bargain hunting, but I'm pretty sure it was unique to her DNA. I recall one particular visit to Honest Ed's, a behemoth old store with signs that warned you not to trip over their low, low prices. It was the perfect setting for us to lose Mother, or perhaps for her to lose us so she could go on a solo scavenger hunt. She sure as hell wasn't concerned about losing us, because during the lengthy time we were separated, never once did we hear her yell for our return. Denise was as calm as a cucumber, while I could already see the headline: "Abandoned Children Found in Honest Ed's Pajama Aisle." We eventually found her where a large display of tin cans had been knocked over and, given the evidence — her tendency to be easily distracted and her proximity to said display — rightfully, deemed her guilty of the crime. Even with the worry of abandonment, I still managed to find a few items I felt were crucial to my existence, but with the kerfuffle caused by the display collapse, the anticipated thrill of Mother agreeing with this assessment went out the window.

She left the store in a good mood, grinning like a Cheshire cat, and not embarrassed in the least by any commotion she'd caused. Evidently, she'd worked up an appetite with the successful mission of finding a proper-fitting bra, which, as per her modus operandi, would eventually be returned to the store. The news of going to Fran's Restaurant for a rare lunch out on the town was music to my ears. Her dereliction of duty, and the worry it caused me, was forgiven once we entered the diner to find a fabulous symphony of clanging dishes and silverware, the alto and baritone ranges of unmelodious diners being led by Conductor Food.

What stays with me of our lunch at Fran's, of course, comes from a child's bird's-eye perspective. The ice in the coke never melts. The heaping pile of piping hot French fries, still glistening with tiny beads of grease, appear on a plate the size of a turkey platter; millions of salt pebbles adorn the drab table-top; and my nose, in close proximity to the plate, still tickles from the vinegar.

There's no possible way to recollect what commercial was airing, but it was taped on a downtown Toronto street in winter. We were unaware of the filming, but can be seen in a split-second frame while walking, Mother in the center, holding our hands. Thinking of the three of us, as a cohesive unit, perhaps on the very day of our outing to Honest Ed's and Fran's, is a rare gem to contemplate.

Daily routines, broken for more than a day, meant we were making our annual pilgrimage to Mother's hometown of Sturgeon Falls. Since the stylish seats of the Dodge Polara mimicked cozy living room sofas, with plenty of room to hang a disco ball, there was little need for dickering and bickering when organizing the simple array of traveling paraphernalia. On the day of departure, we'd shuffle into the car much earlier than any sensible rooster would rouse to herald the morning. The distance, as the crow flies, is posted at roughly three hundred and fifteen miles.

My parents would chain smoke with the windows rolled up, unable to see us clearly through the dense cloud. Mother, after a few hours on the road, would appear to be in a rare, much-needed state of Zen. She'd start singing the French song "Dominique," and we'd proudly belt out the chorus in mangled foreign babble while Dad, his eyes fixed on the road, played the part of stoic chauffeur.

Typically, relatives would toast our safe arrival by opening a prized bottle of homemade dandelion wine. Being from the concrete jungle of the city, the crackling firewood under a corn-filled cauldron, along with meat cooking on the grill mere yards away from the serene river's edge seemed almost too perfect a scene to absorb. In rhythmic intervals, aromatic puffs of smoke mingled with fresh northern air and tickled our cheeks.

On the adjacent property lived an old man whose rustic little cabin was obscured by nature's masterful disarrangement of trees mingled with scruffy greenery. Dad, who made it a point to visit whenever we went to Sturgeon Falls, referred to him simply as "the breadman." Kids were never allowed inside the cabin (probably because the breadman offered spirits of a different sort than those in Mother's powdered milk), but I pictured someone lonely with nothing other than a cot and oven, wandering down to the water to catch a fish for evening supper while waiting for the loaves to rise. I cannot say whether this was an accurate assessment of the breadman's existence, but I do hope that he was showered in praise for his exemplary bread-making talent. I recall wolfing down what Dad brought back, and nothing, sweet Jesus, can compare to a loaf of bread made with loving hands. A swatch of broken bread was, hands down, my favourite thing to grasp, and it still would be years later when handed down the

GF edict, that, if adhered to, would prevent me from enjoying *real* bread ever again.

Nanny's house was chilly in the mornings, with the exception of the kitchen which was heated by the large, wood-burning stove she lit before the rest of us were awake. In the kitchen cupboards, there was always caramel sauce on a shelf where we could reach it and, believe me, it was a sinfully indulgent treat. She'd prepare our toast on the hot cast iron burner, slathering it with the gooey confection — the perfect start to a day that, once we'd eaten, was ours to do as we pleased.

The idea of walking up the dirt road to a hidden pool with water still frigid from the blanket of night was always a little unsettling, especially when the morning air still had a bite to it. But the sun would be warming things up, burning the dew off the lush foliage in the yard, and I'd shake off the worry of being alone with Denise by focusing instead on the exhilaration of bravely getting submerged in the water.

Why we were allowed to go to the pool unaccompanied is a mystery. City folk would have thought it a mere swimming hole. It was made of concrete, but the water was murky, and I'd avoid paying attention to the algae-covered walls and debris floating about from the trees. Ironically, even though I'm older and wiser, without a snorkel, the possibility exists that I'd still panic over some unforeseen calamity and drown. Water, and what's potentially lurking at the muddy bottom, can trigger a tsunami of irrational thoughts.

There are threads that connected the visits up north, regardless of how few and far between they were. It was the occasions when stories, some whispered folklore, were reminisced over as food and drink became the oars that propelled the evening forward into the godless wee hours of foggy mornings. A still-damp tabletop, seen at just below eye level, was proof the night existed — strewn with evidence of a raucous conclusion to the gathering.

The only "big" excursion the four of us took together was a road trip to Expo '67 in Montreal (compliments of E. L. Ruddy, Dad's employer). The highlight of the trip was a fancy dinner, and since this was the one and only occasion to do so as a family, you can imagine how charming it felt.

The restaurant had an entranceway with two doors, one for the main floor eatery and the other for the second floor. The maître d' arrived and conveyed with hand signals and winks that the main floor dining room was more appropriate for little girls. Thinking back, I can only assume the service upstairs at this downtown Montreal eatery served eye-appealing entrees that didn't necessarily involve the food, and a much larger gratuity was expected. Oh my!

Even on the main floor, the staff were resplendently out-fitted in black tuxedos. As our waiter deftly set down my plate, with proper formality, the sleeve of his jacket and the impeccably white, stiffly starched cloth draped over his arm hovered quite close to my face. And, because he was catering to *me*, there was a little embarrassment at being the focus of his professional tending, but there was no lack of composure as my focus quickly zeroed in on the feast before me.

Denise and I were served chicken and French fries in baskets lined with paper, which does seem at odds with the classiness of the place, but they likely knew how to best cater to young girls who certainly didn't belong upstairs.

The day was distinct. Mother wasn't wearing her zippered housedress and Dad wasn't wearing his sleeveless white undershirt, so they were barely recognizable to me. Maybe in those few hours, they were over-the-moon happy, swooning from the novelty of possibly being looked upon as a stylish, modern couple out on the town. The magic of the evening unfolded as they relaxed with their Cointreaus – to me, a scene as rare as spotting Peruvian Spider Monkeys working as sous chefs. The food, as always, was the unifying element.

"I am going to learn to make bread tomorrow, so you may imagine me with my sleeves rolled up, mixing flour, milk, saleratus, etc., with a great deal of grace. I advise you if you don't know how to make the staff of life to learn with dispatch."

~Emily Dickinson

Important Note on Flour

When baking GF, you are trying to produce a result that will mimic the texture and flavour of products made with gluten-containing flour. This is why many recipes call for a combination of GF alternative flours — each has unique characteristics that, when combined, create something decently edible. A recipe can also call for binders such as guar gum (a plant of the pea family) or xanthan gum (a substance produced by bacterial fermentation).

One of the more common GF flours is tapioca, which is derived from the root of a cassava plant, and I'm singling it out because you'll find it listed as either "tapioca flour" or "tapioca starch." The type of refined tapioca flour used in GF baking is not the same as tapioca granules, which are generally used as thickeners in puddings, sauces, et cetera.

Apart from the various GF flours such as rice, tapioca, arrowroot, quinoa, potato, et cetera, you can also purchase GF "all-purpose" flour. All-purpose GF flours are meant for more general use and, depending on the manufacturer, there are countless variations of ingredients that might be used in their formulation.

Don't be fooled into thinking an all-purpose GF flour is the same as an all-purpose *regular* flour. An attempt to use the former to make eggroll wrappers, for example, will be a grave disappointment. You simply cannot expect the same result when the elasticity from gluten matters. On the other hand, if you're adding all-purpose GF flour to, say, a meat mixture, or using it for breading, it won't be noticeable.

The GF white bread recipe that I've been using since 2008 is decently good, but Dad's dear old breadman friend would probably have balked at the ingredients and prep method. Unlike the version I started off with, there's less sugar, which is good, because most GF breads are too sweet. It's simple to make, and the results are consistent. It can be served fresh out of the oven without toasting; otherwise it needs to be refrigerated or frozen, and then toasted. Make sure your ingredients are fresh, especially the yeast. Don't ask me why, but your bread will turn out better if you bake it on a sunny day!

This bread doesn't require kneading. Once it's mixed, it

will be quite gooey and needs to be spooned into the pans. It shouldn't be watery or pourable, but it certainly won't resemble regular dough that can be formed into a ball for kneading.

GF Bread

(Adapted from a recipe found at celiac.com)

Ingredients *(Be sure to use exact measurements)*

In a small bowl combine:

½ cup warm water

2 tsp white sugar

4 tsp dry yeast granules (Traditional or quick-acting granules work fine)

Set timer for 15 minutes

In a medium-sized bowl combine:

1½ cups water

4 tbsp melted butter

1 tsp of apple cider or regular vinegar

3 large eggs

In a large stainless-steel mixing bowl combine:

2 cups of white rice flour

2 cups of tapioca flour

2 tbsp white sugar

4 tsp of xanthan gum

⅔ cup powdered dry milk granules

2 tsp of salt

Directions

When the timer goes off, combine both bowls of wet ingredients into the large bowl of dry ingredients. Mix on high with a hand-held electric mixer for two minutes (I use a Cuisinart hand mixer with dough hooks).

Separate your dough into two equal parts and put into greased bread pans to rise in a warm, draft-free spot. I use Becel margarine to grease, but a GF cooking spray is also an option. "Baking" spray has flour in the formulation, so read your label if gluten is an issue.

Bread may take as long as an hour to rise depending on the yeast used, but once it's risen, bake at 350°F for approximately 35-40 minutes or until it's golden brown and sounds hollow when you tap it. Turn loaves onto a rack to cool.

<u>Brazilian Queijo Buns</u>

(Adapted from a recipe found at allrecipes.com)

These buns are the center of my "bread" universe and I can't live without them. Thank goodness they call for only a few ingredients and are quick to whip up. I vastly prefer them to other GF bun products, especially for holding burger patties, smoked meat, et cetera, because they won't crumble or fall apart. They also have "nooks and crannies" so the butter can swirl about!

I'll admit upfront that I think you need to add flavour to the basic recipe as it's provided from the website. With my adaptation, I use dried onion soup, and spinach (a frozen cube added to the wet ingredients, or fresh chopped added to the dry) – a must, in my opinion.

You can let your imagination run wild and add ingredients such as herbs, minced onion, grated cheddar cheese, and so on.

*Once the buns are out of the oven, I let them cool, slice in half, and then toast before serving. Due to their chewy texture, even when freshly baked, you should **always toast** until you have a good brown crusting on the outside and edges! They also freeze beautifully.*

Wet Ingredients

½ cup olive oil

⅓ cup water

⅓ cup milk

1 tsp salt

1 frozen spinach ball, thawed, if not using fresh

Dry Ingredients

2 cups tapioca flour

2 handfuls of finely minced spinach, if not using frozen

2 tbsp (GF) dry onion soup mix

Any additional herbs, seasoning, or grated cheese, as desired

Final Addition After Mixture Rests

2 large eggs at room temperature

¾ cup grated Parmesan cheese, a little more if batter is too wet

Directions

Preheat oven to 375°F. Bring wet ingredients to a boil, and then remove from heat immediately. Add to dry ingredients and stir well. Let batter sit for fifteen minutes. Add eggs and cheese, and mix well. I slide my (silicone) spatula under the mixture, while folding it over the top, to ensure all dry ingredients are incorporated.

The batter is quite mushy, so I use the spatula to drop the mounds of batter onto the pan, and then roughly shape each one with my buttered fingertips. The buns will rise in the oven, and I don't want them to be too high, so they'll fit into the toaster.

Bake on an ungreased metal sheet pan until they're golden brown and sound hollow when tapped. I get 5-6 buns from the recipe, depending on how big I need them to be. My buns are ready in 25-30 minutes.

<u>Queijo Pizza Crust</u>

Follow the recipe above, with preheated oven set at 375°F.

I put aside enough of the dough for two buns, which I'll bake. This leaves me with the perfect amount of dough for a standard size, round, 13" pizza pan.

For pizza crust, grease the pan, and then spread the dough with oiled or buttered fingertips. Bake about ten minutes, or until the dough is starting to set. As it's baking, poke any bubbles that pop up. If it's not set enough it will be too soft to remove from pan. If it's left in too long, the crust may be too crunchy, so keep an eye on it.

This step is a must: Remove pan from the oven, then loosen the crust from the pan before dressing. Carefully slide a stiff spatula under a loose corner (I hold my spatula backwards so the edge is facing the pan), and gently scrape to loosen it. The dough is pliable and this is very easy to do.

Oil the pan again and set the crust back on it. Rub the crust with olive oil, and dress (sauce, toppings, and cheese, as desired). Return to oven to finish baking.

<u>Queijo Appetizers</u>

Use the same recipe with the oven preheated at 375°F.

Grease a 17"x12" rectangular baking pan, or any other large pan, so the appetizer crust will be thin. With your fingers oiled or buttered, spread the entire dough. I like to take a knife and roughly divide it to make either two or four sections. If you prefer, you can bake it as one large crust then divide it once it's removed from the oven.

Bake for about ten minutes, or, until the dough is set enough to remove from pan, using the same method for the pizza crust to remove it.

Drizzle olive oil over the dough. I then sprinkle with freshly minced garlic, or garlic I've baked with thyme, and then mashed. In a pinch you can use garlic powder or omit it altogether.

I will top each half (or quarter) section with a different type of cheese — Buffalo mozzarella, bocconcini, mozzarella al Fresca, or Feta. Alternatively, you can simply use grated mozzarella on all of them.

One section might have thinly sliced heirloom tomatoes, thinly sliced Vidalia onion, fresh basil leaves, and chopped prosciutto; another might have kalamata olives, thinly sliced mushrooms, and ham. The dressing options are only limited to your imagination.

I sprinkle all of them with Parmigiano Reggiano, oregano, and chili flakes.

Before serving, return the queijos to the oven set at 375°F to finish baking. Once the cheese is nice and bubbly, they're ready.

These appetizers are simply wonderful, and actually quite effortless to make.

Grace's Italian Butter

Grace's butter is very versatile. It's great as a base to use before topping the Queijo appetizers, or as a rub for meats, like pork tenderloin, before barbequing.

Ingredients

Using a blender or coffee grinder, combine the following:

1 tbsp crushed red pepper flakes

1 tbsp black peppercorns

1½ tbsp dried oregano

1 tbsp dried rosemary

1½ tbsp dried basil

1 tbsp garlic powder

1½ tbsp dried parsley

1½ tbsp fresh minced garlic

¾ tsp salt

Once combined, add ¼ cup extra virgin olive oil and stir. Seal in airtight jar and refrigerate.

GF French Bread

This recipe was found at food.com and was posted by GlutenFreeGirl. It's the first GF baguette I've attempted making since 2007, and it's good, especially for garlic bread or bruschetta.

Ingredients

2 cups rice flour (white)

1 cup tapioca flour

3 tsp xanthan gum

1½ tsp salt

2 tsp egg substitute (optional)

2 tbsp sugar

1½ cups lukewarm water

2 tbsp fast rise yeast

2 tbsp butter or margarine, melted

3 egg whites, beaten lightly

1 tsp vinegar

Melted butter for brushing, optional

Directions

In the bowl of a heavy-duty mixer, place flours, xanthan gum, salt and egg replacer (if using).

In a small bowl, dissolve the sugar in the water and add yeast. (I add the water last as it mixes better.)

Wait until the yeast mixture foams slightly, then blend into dry ingredients. (I set timer for 15 minutes.)

Add the butter, egg whites and vinegar. Beat on high for 3 minutes (I use my handheld Cuisinart with dough hook attachments.)

To form loaves, spoon dough onto greased cornmeal-dusted cookie sheet in two long French-loaf shapes or spoon into special French bread pans. (I love cornmeal in some applications, but prefer omitting it. Personally, the bread is great and doesn't need the crunchiness from the baked cornmeal.)

Slash diagonally every few inches. If desired, brush with melted butter.

Cover the dough and let rise in a warm place untiled doubled in bulk, 20-25 minutes.

Preheat oven to 400°F. Bake for 40-45 minutes. (My loaves are ready in 30 minutes.)

Remove from pan to cool.

V.6

"Ultimately, we are all products of the experiences we have and the decisions we make as children, and it remains a peculiar detail of human condition that something as precious as the future is entrusted to us when we possess so little foresight. Perhaps that's what makes hindsight so intriguing. When you're young the future is a blank canvas, but looking back you are always able to see the big picture."

~Simon Pegg

Our kitchen had the potential to suit any cook, but instead it was more of a no-nonsense utility room with stark white walls. On one side, there was the classic style Formica kitchen table wrapped with a stainless-steel band and four vinyl chairs, and, across the room, a matching miniature set sat in front of the iron water heater (Denise's liver graveyard located underneath it). Above our little table, the window looked out onto the grand old dame of a maple tree in the side yard.

Once old enough, I took on the role of Chief Dishwasher, so the lion's share of kitchen duties ate up an unfortunate chunk of my time. It's a pity there was nothing stimulating in the room to entertain me during the tedious cleanup, other than a chintzy little plaque that hung above the doorway. In a predominately Italian neighbourhood of Catholic faith, where God had more star power than Elvis (houses were filled with endless arrays of eye-popping trinkets to prove it), that plaque was the closest thing to a religious artifact we had. Clearly, it was an indication that a non-practising Protestant was paying the rent.

There are a few slight variations of the poem, and the author is listed as Unknown. I guarantee you that I'm the only one who left that house with the ditty engrained on the brain.

The sage message it conveyed went like this:

Thank God for Dirty Dishes

They Have A Tale to Tell

While Others May Go Hungry

We're Eating Very Well

With Home, Health, and Happiness

We Shouldn't Want to Fuss

By the Stack of Evidence

God's Been Very Good to Us!

Green Acres was a sitcom centred on Oliver, a New York City lawyer who decided to take up farming. He and his high-society wife (fittingly played by the spicily seductive Eva Gabor), moved from Manhattan to a farm in Hooterville where they lived with their pig, Arnold Ziffel, whom I adored. To say Oliver's wife was having trouble adapting to country life is an understatement. After dinner, she'd gather up the ends of the tablecloth, which was still laden with dirty dishes, mind you, and toss it all out the window. Had we a good stock of plates and silverware, there's no doubt I'd have attempted to do the same.

I always loathed this chore, but never more so than when it coincided with the approach of sunset. At that time of day when multi-hued low-lying clouds deepened in colour, resembling swatches of playdough rolled into thin strips. It was mandatory to squeeze every last second out of a delightful day, and I'd work double-time at my task, ever mindful that legions of bats were hiding in the shadows, waiting to swoop down precisely at dusk with a plan to fly off with my entire scalp of hair.

One summer, after enduring my tortured and protracted pleas, my parents finally relented and purchased for me the latest fashion fad. God knows what they went without, and what Denise went without by unselfishly accommodating (or, more accurately, muzzling) me — but there I was, the only sharpie-do-kid on the block with a brand-spanking-new pair of white Go-Go boots, and by God, they were going to be put to good use until the last glimmer of daylight left the sky.

Wearing those boots provided an extremely rare occasion where feeling suave and confident suited me. Never mind that my frame was a bit stocky (perhaps one or two meatballs over quota), or that my standard issue haircut looked as though Mother used a bowl to guide the scissors (Was she trained for this task on an army base?), any big-shot teenagers who dared to compete against me surely would've regretted looking like they were born with two left feet.

My routine was centred on Nancy Sinatra's "These Boots Are Made For Walking," and whenever I wasn't chained to the sink I could be found flailing about on the front lawn, pretty sure that with enough practice I might be discovered by a passerby and booked on the Ed Sullivan Show. My personal claim to fame was the Sullivan surname, and, surely to God, Ed would welcome my appearance, as it was entirely possible we were related. If you're familiar with the refrain of the song (or are curious enough to Google it), you'll see how perfect it was for an elaborately dramatic presentation in my equally dramatic boots.

Despite my valiant efforts, by summer's end it was apparent that the only way I'd see Ed Sullivan's stage was on the screen of our black and white. There was disappointment felt at the myopia of my fellow citizens (Didn't they recognize a diamond in the rough when they saw one?), but on my first day of school fate had finally dealt me a proper hand. Ballet classes were to be held in the evening! When the school bell rang at the end of the day, I tore home at breakneck speed, the application form doing pirouettes in the wind. Looking back, I can more fully appreciate how Mother balanced her usual pragmatism with kindness by allowing me to take a few lessons they could ill afford.

Mother already knew — a dancer I was not. There was no pleasure to be found hanging onto a wooden bar for dear life, twisted like a pretzel, while the Russian Tulip, losing patience with me, orbited about like Sputnik. Thank God she wasn't instructed to buy me a tutu before the lessons started; if she had, I'd have been forced into the child labour market in two shakes of a rat's tail.

Mother didn't use the experience as a teachable moment by telling me that, although I'd failed at this, I could find another, more suitable artistic outlet. She didn't need to. As the saying goes, "Silence speaks volumes," and the message was received. Looking back, it's obvious there was always a need to pursue creative endeavours, trying to find the one meant for me. My stubbornness has derailed me at times, but my spunkiness has propelled me to find what I was looking for and make peace with its importance, or lack thereof, in the grand scheme of things.

Apart from the dance lessons, there was no enrollment in extra-curricular activities, so my focus was on the classroom. At the beginning of each schoolyear, nothing was more exciting than inhaling the smell of musty, well-worn pages in my new, old books that needed to be carefully protected by cutting up brown paper shopping bags to be folded and made into covers. I'd proudly marvel at my new, old desk, with various carvings on the wooden top and gobs of chewing gum adhered to its underbelly. If at all possible, I would've dragged that desk home with me each night.

The Catholic school was segregated by gender until integration. Girls were required to wear black, bibbed tunics with the skirt portion crisply pleated, and a white shirt. Memories are vivid of Mother sending me to the corner store for milk, and experiencing the wrath of her fury, if the waxy exterior of the milk carton got a bit sweaty on the way home and marked my tunic.

The nuns, who taught the girls, appeared sternly author-itative and yet divinely goddess-like as they hurriedly flitted about, floor-length black habits swooshing and swirling, their long, dangling crosses flapping harmoniously in rhythm. I was positively awestruck with one particularly youthful sister, until she posted a chart on the blackboard with a depiction of souls, one for each pupil. She warned us that any sin or wrongdoing committed would result in a black pebble being drawn in. My personal interpretation was quite simple. Once the soul was filled with black pebbles, I was going to hell, with no turning back. This was an irrevocable situation, and surely something to worry over for my entire existence on earth, albeit, likely a short one. Most days I cannot remember by supper what I've eaten for breakfast, but I'll never forget the picture of a soul with my name on it (I draw a blank though, at the accumulated pebble count!).

Outside the classroom, lessons in preparation for life were pretty scarce. Over the years, a motley crew of extended relatives congregated in the kitchen – not a particularly ideal spot for a harp, but well suited for a banjo. It was a benefit to be nosy, especially when something out of the blue was discovered. There was the uncle who famously turned road-kill into delectable meals, and bless Dad for warning us to never ask what type of meat he was serving, for the sake of our sanity. Mind you, with this revelation, I'd have preferred Dad's offering of a glass of water and a toothpick, his standard response to a complaint of being hungry. There was the burly little uncle, an exact replica of a garden gnome, who slaved over his pot of corned beef hash, which, no doubt, was a recipe passed along to him from his wife who spent many years in the famous kitchen of a Montreal diner. Now this was something worth noticing – the result of his labour was so successful, I'd sustain my life with the hash, by slathering it onto fresh bread until the last speck of it was gone.

There were no time-honoured secret family recipes or quirky rituals recorded from that kitchen on Northcliffe, and the wonderful Italian food that was nourishing my psyche, courtesy of the neighbourhood signoras, didn't come with recipes attached, and another family's traditions, of course, were never taught and not mine for the taking. How on earth the hash concoction was made remains a mystery, but, with the memory of taste, I was able to decently recreate a few of my favourite Italian dishes.

In contradictory fashion, there were a few isolated instances when instructions were offered. My aunt taught me to smoke and blow smoke rings. It's too bad I was such a compliant student and couldn't see the bigger picture. And a great-uncle wisely instructed, "You must chew each bite of food one-hundred times before swallowing for proper digestion." He was quite elderly and carried himself with the solemnity of a statesman — posture, attire, and manners, all impeccable — and he attributed this advice to his longevity. Although it sounded like a simple task in theory, in practice it was grueling to adopt. Looking back, in this case, I'm sorry I wasn't a compliant student, considering the digestion issues I deal with now.

The bit of embarrassment that I experienced during our special family dinner in Montreal was apparently the prelude of perils that lay ahead when shyness is also an affliction. In the early years of our marriage, Claude and I were out for dinner and seated at a crowded table when I popped a chunk of bacon-wrapped filet mignon in my mouth, only to realize the meats were held together with a toothpick. With the need to always be polite, long ago ingrained, and not wanting anyone see me pull it out of my mouth, my split-second decision was to chew the hell out of it and hope for the best. It was better, in my opinion, to risk choking to death. It's also notable, that my compliance with great-uncle's chewing habit had lasted less than a couple of days, hardly long enough to learn the knack of chewing and swallowing toothpicks like a pro.

Another tidbit of advice that captivated me came from my godmother, dispensed over the course of a memorable lunch where we were served matzoh ball soup. She advised that our departure date is predetermined and the ticket is printed on the day we're born. She had a wicked sense of humour, but I had no idea if she was trying to be funny when I heard this morsel of eternal wisdom. Her intent was to comfort me so I'd stop worrying about things out of my control; instead, it would eventually become the best excuse one could hope for when justifying the continuation of a smoking habit – another irony that wasn't lost on me.

One of my favourite childhood songs, in hindsight, was quite fitting. "There's a Hole in the Bottom of the Sea." *There's a hole in the bottom of the sea, there's a log in the hole, there's a bump on a log, there's a frog on the bump, there's a wart on the frog, there's a fly on the wart, and there's a flea on the fly.* What a perfect way to describe the ever-growing compilation of behaviours that seemed so inconsequential at the time but would be finding their way into baggage that was outfitted with sturdy wheels, needed for easy take-along navigation.

V.7

~George Miller

*T*he neighbourhood vibe was mighty alluring to me, like a welcoming porchlight to a moth on a chilly evening. Whenever I stepped outside, I'd immediately be greeted by the aromas that wafted out the doors of our Italian neighbours, which created a patchwork veil that blanketed the entire neighbourhood. But those aromas implied hard work. The signora across the street would be wearing her husband's huge unlaced work boots, making trip after trip to the curb, dragging one bushel after another to the house. Tomatoes and grapes were squirrelled away into a cavernous dark basement, morphing after tedious labour into wonderful wall-to-wall rows of freshly jarred sauce and bottled wine. On a production day, the aromas were so pervasive, it made my heart thump with joy. The idea of having to go home at some point was a dreaded prospect.

There were starkly different internal workings in our kitchen compared to those of our neighbours. Dinner preparation at our house was an exacting science: all ingredients cut with surgical precision, no experimentation allowed, no inspiration required. Next door, the lively kitchen almost seemed festive. Signora and Nonna bustled about preparing dinners that may have been a dreaded routine to them but to me were something of beauty. This was not mere sustenance, but manna from heaven. How could it not be? There was no recipe book required, just an innate sense of how to do good things with a few simple ingredients.

Before the crack of dawn, the neighbourhood men would slip away to toil as labourers; a strapping lot they were. At the pantry window while waiting for Dad's arrival, I watched as they returned home each night — with deeply burnished faces, every wrinkle embedded with sooty dirt, feet dragging as if their work boots were lined with concrete, and always in brooding silence. Maybe they were daydreaming of their homeland, where merry beams of sunlight bounce off ancient cobblestones, across lush rolling fields, through well-tended olive groves, and into the village square, where men play bocce with vino in hand. The thing is, I didn't want to *watch* the neighbourhood men return home — instead, I wanted to wait for their return at their house, in their kitchen, with their family. Pining for this, while Mother fancied up the starchy boiled potatoes (puh–day-doe-s, as she pronounced them with her lingering French intonation) by putting them through the ricer.

At this time of day Mother had dinner well underway, and what would be served was dictated solely by what day of the week it was. Unless we had company, there was no practical reason to stray from the schedule, so weekly dinner routines stayed pretty much the same. If God had only created an eighth day, she might've attempted to whip up salmon patties like the ones Aunt Dot made as Denise and I adored them. We equally adored Aunt Hazel's tea biscuits that she'd bring over fresh from the oven, along with a bag of store-bought cookies covered in minty chocolate. Managing the requisite *hello* without looking overly rambunctious to get at the goods was a noble feat.

Most dinner invitations to a neighbour's house were extended informally, which is to say I'd be waved in at the last minute by one of the kids. I'd slink in, praying that in all the commotion my presence would go unnoticed by the adults. Of course, this wasn't the case, and when Signora inevitably spotted me and nodded her approval, the relief made me giddy. Being at the table "officially" was as divine to me as Father Polito's visits were to Mother.

Dinner consisted of freshly plucked arugula-type greens doused in olive oil, customarily grown from Italian heirloom seeds; steaming chicken broth (lovingly referred to as "Italian penicillin") with floating acini de pepe; pasta with tomato sauce; and crusty bread which was never sliced but properly torn, each ruggedly broken piece showing off its own unique pattern of caverns. And, can you imagine my delight when homemade red wine was poured into small glasses! This was bewildering, coming from a house where, if powdered milk didn't suit the palate, water was on tap.

I'd make good use of my time while there, consuming enough pasta (rigatoni was my favourite) to hold me for a week, but in my case, it just wasn't possible to actually get full. The only words I can guarantee were never spoken at Signora's were "No thank you, I've had enough."

Early on, I devised strict Rules, the adherence to which was necessary in order to ensure my continued presence:

- Never look unsure by sniffing or frowning if something foreign is introduced. (This was rarely the case, but one must be prepared for every eventuality.)

- Accept a second helping with a show of deep gratitude, by going cross-eyed when swallowing.

- Every last bite must be eaten with the same measure of reverence as depicted in the painting of the Apostles at the Last Supper, which, by the way, hung above the well-worn wooden kitchen table. *Grazie, grazie!*

The master of the house, the burly signor, always seemed to be seething with what appeared to be a lot of pent-up something or other. It was unsettling and surely should've deterred me to shy away, but I'd abandon any justifiable fear because, simply put, his own vulnerability was palpable. It was unspoken, but clearly understood, that Nonna, being the elder woman in the house, was the one whom everyone rightfully feared. So, *per favore Signor*, consider my deepest gratitude when determining the size of my serving!

Most men had a widowed nonna – either their own mother or their mother-in-law – living under their roof. They must have inherently understood the natural pecking order of things: hard work would drive men into the ground, and then their widowed wives would morph into mystical Nonnas, and the circle of life would continue. This is all highly speculative, but the theory fits well with my recollection.

Every nonna looked the same: elf-like in stature, hunched over from years of tedious tending, and cloaked in black, which starkly contrasted their tightly woven white hair. Canes were threatening sorts of weapons but were probably nothing other than antique olive branches brought over from the Motherland. Their decisive gait looked painful but resolute as they marched along, and sufficiently explained why the sidewalks had cracks. Kids never dared to walk on those cracks, and to this day I still try to avoid them out of nostalgic habit.

The neighbourhood kids warned me that their nonnas could curse me with an Evil Eye (aka "the Malocchio") which was more than a little troublesome. Other than the bad connotations it implied, it was impossible to know what type of unacceptable behaviour would cause me to be afflicted, or how the curse would manifest itself, but the last bloody thing a kid like me needed was to experience the Godforsaken curse firsthand.

In the presence of nonnas, my behaviour was exceptional, and I'm pleased to say that it was clear they approved of my plumpness, unlike the rather lean bambinos in their own houses. Often, a bony little hand reached towards my face to pinch my cheek, without a word spoken. When no spell had been cast, it was a tremendous relief, but I'd still feel a bit spooked. To sleep fitfully after an encounter, at bedtime, I'd triple check the bedroom closet door was firmly shut to ensure the lurking ghosts remained contained.

The ancient Evil Eye spell belief is complex and not exclusive to Italian culture. It's safe to say, in rudimentary terms, that jealousy, envy, or dislikes are examples of what can bring a curse upon you. Water equates to life, dryness to death, so the curse will dry up liquids. A curse might be diagnosed by dripping olive oil into a basin of water to determine if it resembles the shape of an eye. After rituals have been performed, if the droplets of oil disperse into a meaningless pattern, it signals the curse has been reversed.

It was shocking when, instead of a curse, I, along with my sister, received a "formal" dinner invitation, and straight from the signor himself. Actually, it was more of a summons than a request, and it would be fair to admit my sense of excitement was barely manageable. I don't recall the reason for the invitation, but it had to have been something quite special. This would be Denise's first and only dinner with the neighbours. She was never interested in food and far too picky to have been lured into any kitchen. There were more foods she disliked than liked, and it was an oddity that she loved raw hamburger meat (she claims it's no grosser than eating beef tartare). Of her many quirks one thing was certain, beef was her thing, and she was in for quite a treat.

This was my first introduction to steak, as it wasn't included in the perpetually revolving menu at our house. On the occasion in question, we arrived and politely joined the feast. The usual salad greens, pasta, bread and wine were present, but the crowning jewel was the presentation of the platter of steak. Signor and Signora, beaming with pride, watched for our appreciative reaction.

Each of us received a workingman's portion of meat, their reasoning obviously being if you're going to treat, treat well. Until this visit, there was never a morsel of food these people set in front of me that couldn't easily be tucked into, but there was a problem.

The steak didn't have that crispy fat that is typically considered delectable; instead, it was blubbery, thick, oily, uncooked fat, clinging, as if for dear life, to each of our pieces. Looking around the table, all were chewing — no, gnawing, actually — and enjoying. Who would dare waste? It would be disrespectful, even foolish; obviously fat was good, as good for you as the meat itself. Under no circumstance was I going to dare risk their disapproval by leaving a speck on my plate, because this was not going to be my last meal in their house. With nudging and nodding a plan was quickly implemented.

One could hope our slight indiscretion had gone unnoticed, but we needed to leave as quickly as possible. We nervously thanked our gracious guests and headed home.

Mother would surely applaud our resourcefulness and no doubt be pleased at our ladylike conduct. However, we'd have to explain why we had dripping, heavy wads of fat in the pockets of her newly designed, hand-knit sweater creations. They were blue with ribbed cuffs, high collars and zippered fronts. The labor involved in making them sufficiently explained why she wasn't exactly thrilled. The nervousness experienced that day is as memorable as the debacle with the knit sweaters and the steak dinner itself.

The anticipation of an Italian birthday party rivalled Christmas celebrations. To my delight, the main course was hot dogs, and I enjoyed them as much as the cake. Buns were a luxury, so the wieners were put on a plain piece of bread. The steam from the wiener made the bread gummy and chewy, compliments of wonderful gluten, and nothing compared. For years I'd eat them this way, thinking it was some sort of "Italian tradition."

And I've never eaten cake since, as decadently drenched in liqueur, impossibly tall or lavishly iced, with pennies, dimes, and nickels mixed into the batter. I wonder now if the coins were washed first because they weren't wrapped, but at the time I'd have gladly picked dried chewing gum from a penny without giving it a moment's thought.

Apart from that one piece of steak and the snail dinners I was never subjected to, everything the neighbours cooked hit the spot. To me, their meals remain the greatest evidence that "It takes a village to raise a child." Or, perhaps more accurately, it took an Italian family to raise Colette. And it wasn't just the food. It seemed as though there was an invisible barrier around their kitchen that made it impenetrable by any negative vibes of financial or cultural struggle, or personal strife.

When news arrived that a beloved signora from my childhood had died, I was truly shaken. How many times had I stared out the kitchen window, watching her? She could only speak Italian, yet mysteriously impacted my life in profound ways. In my mind she's still alive — haggard and humble in manner, with chafed hands, twinkling eyes, and a broad smile exposing her missing teeth — her aura, one of shy, girlish innocence. Most of all, I remember the quiet strength, based on the teachings of God and a commitment to her marriage and children, that had allowed her to leave behind the land of her birth and forge a new life in her adopted country.

Aunt Dot's Salmon Patties

Ingredients

1 tin of salmon, drained (Cousin Maureen says her mom crushed the bones for the calcium content, but it's a matter of preference.)

1 egg

1 onion, finely diced

1 stalk of celery, finely diced

Dash of dill weed and cracked pepper

Enough (GF) breadcrumbs to form a nice patty

Directions

Mix together and form patties. Refrigerate patties for a few hours before cooking in a lightly oiled non-stick frying pan. Pat patties with paper towel upon removal.

Homemade Mayo

Delicious with Aunt Dot's salmon patties or homemade French fries!

Ingredients

1 large, fresh, clean, store bought egg that's been properly processed and refrigerated — bring to room temperature

1 tbsp Dijon mustard

1 tbsp white wine vinegar

½ tsp salt

1 tsp freshly squeezed lemon juice

1 cup sunflower oil

Directions

Using a hand-held immersion blender, whisk the egg in a small glass or ceramic bowl. Add in the mustard, vinegar, salt, and lemon juice, and continue blending until the egg yolk has lightened in colour. Slowly stream in a few drops of oil at a time for the first ½ cup of oil. Initially adding the oil in drops, slowly, is critical for emulsion. As the mixture begins to thicken, you can add the remaining oil in a thin stream until it's completely incorporated and the mayo is light and fluffy.

Variations: Be creative and add fresh herbs, or relish (Bick's Gourmet Relish is fabulous) and paprika for tartar sauce when making fish.

Note: To check if an egg is fresh, set it into a container of water. If it's standing upright or floats to the top, discard it – or use it for ammunition. Just don't eat it!

<u>Aunt Hazel's Wonderful Tea Biscuits</u>

For those of you who can tolerate gluten, I wanted to include this delightful recipe for biscuits just as my aunt would have made them.

Ingredients *(use exact)*

2 cups all-purpose flour (with gluten)

3 tsp baking powder

½ tsp salt

½ cup Crisco shortening

1-2 tbsp sugar, depending on your sweet tooth

1 egg

1 cup of milk

Directions

Mix everything together lightly except egg and milk. (Cousin Nancy thinks her biscuits aren't as good as her mom's because she tends to over mix.)

Put egg in one-cup measure, fill with milk, and lightly stir. Pour into mixture quickly and blend with knife.

Pat into circles and bake in oven preheated at 450°F for approximately fifteen minutes (depending on oven), until golden brown.

Spinach Salad

Spinach salad is the centerpiece of almost every dinner. Everyone claims they cannot make their salad to taste like mine, even though it's really a simple salad to make. Maybe mine tastes unique because I've got the "eye-ball-wrist-shake" measurement down to a science, and they like the flavour of my oil and vinegar.

I use baby spinach topped with a little arugula (my kids prefer just the spinach), thinly sliced Vidalia onion (sweet or red if it's not in season). Good quality extra-virgin olive oil, aged balsamic vinegar, and Parmigiano Reggiano are added one at a time, just before we eat. The tossing is a ritual, and the salad is alive and fresh with this method.

At Signora's house the salad bowl was almost as big as the table and for good reason. It's a nutritionally solid foundation to build a dinner around.

Pasta Sauce

This is my inauthentic version of pasta sauce. There are countless ways I can alter the sauce (for example, sometimes, when whipping up a small sauce for two, I'll forgo the ribs and sauté minced onion with fresh garlic, parsley and oregano, and then simmer with canned heirloom tomatoes), but I never go too far astray. I often lightly fry hot Italian sausage to render excess fat, and then add them to the sauce to simmer with the ribs. If fresh basil is available, I'll shred a bunch by hand and add before serving.

Ingredients

2 tbsp regular olive oil

Partial rack of pork ribs (6-8 bones)

1½ cup dry red wine, or more as desired.

4-5 garlic cloves, minced

2-28 oz. cans San Marzano tomatoes, pureed with handheld emulsion blender

1 large canned tomato juice, 48 oz.

1 can tomato sauce, if desired. This will make sauce thicker so use if simmering time is an issue

2 tbsp dried basil, or more to taste

1½ tbsp dried oregano, or more to taste

½ tbsp dried rosemary, or more to taste, optional

½ tbsp crushed red peppers, or more to taste

2 tsp salt

Freshly cracked pepper to taste

Fresh chopped green and/or red pepper, onion, and fresh mushrooms, all optional

½ cup grated Parmesan cheese

Parmigiana Reggiano for grating on top, if you'd like

Directions

In a large Dutch Oven, heat olive oil over medium heat until hot but not smoking. Add ribs and braise until golden brown, and then spoon out any excess oil from pot.

Add wine and simmer a few minutes while picking up bits of seared meat. Add the garlic, tomatoes, and tomato juice with all other remaining ingredients. Reduce and simmer for several hours. It's even better if you have time make it a day ahead and reheat. Adjust seasoning according to taste.

I remove the ribs when the meat is falling off the bone and serve it on the platter with whatever other meats I might be serving.

<u>Meatballs</u>

I always thought my meatballs were fabulous, but as it turns out it took Claude forty years to admit that they're tasty but not as moist as they could be. Mamma Mia, I was on a mission to figure out how to optimize moistness.

Because I make meatballs in large batches, the countless trial runs needed to find an accurate recipe resulted in the production of hundreds of balls (Santa could've used them to stuff all the Christmas stockings in Whoville). Thankfully, Claude was willing to sample the test balls from each batch in pasta sauce, but he equally enjoyed them with fried onions and mushrooms in brown gravy and a side of mashed potatoes (good thing he walks two hours a day, faithfully). They're also fabulous on a baguette with pasta sauce and melted mozzarella.

The recipe is a bit unusual, and you might balk at it, but the balance of seasoning, and the moistness, suits me. If dairy is an issue, you can omit it, however, you might need to make adjustments to maintain the moistness I've been able to achieve with a meatball that is delicate but holds its form well when cooking. I realize adding water seems asinine, but it's a secret trick for many famous Italian chefs and home cooks. I was terrified at the thought of using it, but would never go back to making them without it. And, again, with a little ingenuity, you can easily adjust the recipe if necessary. I'll get approximately forty meatballs, which I freeze once cooled so they're readily available.

Note: Many recipes call for soaking stale Italian bread in milk, which would be my preference if gluten wasn't an issue. Throughout my countless trials, I used GF breadcrumbs but the brands available were too hard and pebbly and clumped in the milk (of course, still an option if you can find a finer GF breadcrumb). I tried a stale GF baguette but it didn't come close to resembling gluten-containing Italian bread, so I settled on good old-fashioned GF crackers, which moistened perfectly in the milk.

Ingredients

2 lbs lean or extra lean ground beef

1 lb ground veal

1 lb ground pork

¾ cup (GF) crackers, crushed

½ cup milk

1 small cooking onion chopped fine

½ of a bunch of fresh Italian parsley, chopped fine — do not use dried!

8 medium-sized garlic cloves, pounded and minced very fine — best method for amount of intenseness suited to this recipe

½ tbsp crushed chilies, or to taste

1½ tbsp dried oregano

1½ tsp anise, crushed using mortar and pestle, more or less to taste (optional)

2¼ tsp salt

Freshly cracked pepper to taste

½ cup grated Parmesan cheese

¾ cup Ricotta cheese

3 eggs fork beaten

⅔ cups warm water

Regular olive oil for cooking

Directions

Combine breadcrumbs and milk in small bowl and set aside.

In a very large mixing bowl, add the meat by taking rotating hunks from each package and gently separating, so it will mingle and more easily blend without being overworked.

Add in the onion, parsley, garlic, seasonings, Parmesan cheese, Ricotta cheese, and eggs. Before adding the milk-soaked bread-crumbs, stir the mixture and make sure the crumbs are mushy and moist. Pour the warm water over everything. Slide your hand under the ingredients and fold upward while turning the bowl, watching to make sure everything is blending, careful to not overwork the mixture to the point of mushiness.

Note: These meatballs will be as moist as any you'll find, which means they'll need to be cooked with care.

Form meatballs to desired size. On medium-high heat, fry in small batches, preferably in a non-stick, or ceramic coated pan

(I use a large Le Creuset non-stick) with 3 tbsp olive oil per batch (or oven bake if it's your preference). Start by gently shaking your pan, while using a silicone spatula to nudge any that are sticking. Once they've cooked enough to form and won't fall apart, use a soup spoon to turn each meatball over. I never overcook my meatballs because they will continue cooking in the sauce. Remove meatballs to a tray lined with paper towel to absorb the excess fat and let cool before bagging, if freezing.

<u>Baked Eggplant – Non-Breaded</u>

Years ago, I avoided eggplant dishes, assuming the eggplant would be bitter, or fishy tasting. Over time, with proper preparation, this casserole has become my hands-down, go-to, most cherished dish, and, when it's served with a spinach salad, it's a great meatless dinner. Since it's made often, my preference is a non-breaded version, which is great, because it's made with little fuss and less calories.

Ingredients

1 purple eggplant

Salt

Olive oil, as much as needed

1 small brick of Gruyere cheese, or other preferred type (6-8 oz.)

Very small pinch of cinnamon (optional)

Oregano, as much as desired

Garlic powder, as much as desired

Crushed chili flakes, as much as desired

Cracked pepper

2-398 ml cans (about 13 oz. each) of high-quality crushed tomatoes — I use Hunts Heirloom.

Directions

Slice eggplant lengthwise (you can also slice in rounds — not too thick), and place pieces on a wire rack. Salt each side and allow them to sit until they've rendered their purple juice — at least thirty minutes per side. Pat each round with dampened paper towel, and then give it a gentle squeeze with dry paper towel. If salt is an issue, rinse and dry well.

Preheat oven to 325°F.

Heat a cast iron skillet on medium-high with 2-3 tbsp olive oil. Sear the eggplant pieces in batches to avoid over-crowding. Remove each piece when it has nicely browned.

Sprinkle a little olive oil into the bottom of a medium-sized cast iron casserole pot and then add a few tbsp of tomato sauce. Sprinkle with desired amount of oregano, garlic powder, crushed chilies, and cinnamon if using.

Set the first layer of eggplant slices into pot. Sprinkle grated cheese over the eggplant. Season with cracked pepper. Cover with tomato sauce. Sprinkle more seasoning and chili flakes. Continue making layers of eggplant, cheese, sauce and seasoning until everything is in the pot.

Cover and bake for about an hour.

You can make eggplant lasagna (using non-breaded or breaded), however you would need to double the recipe above. Lightly oil your lasagna pan and cover the bottom with a thin layer of pasta sauce. Place eggplant over the sauce; then add a layer of ricotta cheese or béchamel sauce or mozzarella, and then add a layer of lasagna noodles and a layer of sauce. Continue making layers. Top with shredded mozzarella, and then bake at 325°F until done.

Veal or Chicken Scallopini

This is a quick dish to make and is nice served with pasta tossed with fresh chopped tomatoes, extra virgin olive oil, a pinch of crushed chilies, and grated Parmigiano Reggiano. You can also serve it with potatoes that are roasted with fresh rosemary and salt.

Ingredients

10 oz. of very thin veal pieces (about 6 thin slices) or 2 small boneless skinless chicken breasts, pounded thin

(GF) All-purpose flour, as much needed for dredging

3 tbsp regular olive oil, per batch

12 button mushrooms or your favourite exotic, sliced

½ cup white wine

2 tbsp capers

¼ cup fresh thyme

½ cup of fresh parsley measured before mincing

3 tbsp butter

Juice of 1 lemon

Salt

Cracked pepper, to taste

Directions

If you haven't purchased thin veal, perhaps labelled as "scallopini," you'll need to place the meat between parchment paper and using the flat side of a mallet, pound until thin, careful that they don't get too thin or they'll fall apart. After pounding the chicken breasts, cut them into manageable sized pieces (you'll get about 6-8 pieces). Sprinkle lightly with salt.

Dredge meat in (GF) flour. In a large saucepan on medium-high, heat the oil until hot but not smoking. In small batches to avoid overcrowding, cook the meat until nicely browned. The chicken will take a little longer than the veal to cook. Remove meat to a pan lined with paper towel.

Reduce heat and add the mushrooms, wine, capers, and herbs. Season with cracked pepper to taste. Simmer gently until reduced by about half.

Incorporate butter and lemon to pan, mix well, and then add meat back in. When serving, top with freshly chopped herbs if desired.

<u>Veal, Chicken or Eggplant Parmesan</u>

The cutlets I dream about from childhood were baked in the oven on a large pan, however, my cutlets are pan fried. This is a good recipe for a family dinner.

Note: It drives me batty if I run out of breading in the middle of coating and cooking, so I prepare enough to get through the process. If I'm only using one eggplant, 2 eggs for the milk wash is plenty. It's easy to adjust the amounts according to your needs.

Meat Ingredients

Veal: 1½ lbs of veal (about 10 thin cutlets)

Chicken: 1½ lbs (2 boneless, skinless chicken breasts once pounded, and cut into workable sized pieces to dip, will usually give me about 6-8 cutlets.)

Eggplant: 1 large eggplant sliced into rounds, salted on both sides, and then set on wire rack for 30 minutes per side, or until they've rendered their juice. Pat each round with dampened paper towel, and then give it a gentle squeeze with dry paper towel. If salt is an issue, rinse and dry well.

Breading Ingredients

Take out 3 good-sized bowls

Bowl # 1: Flour

½ cup (GF) all-purpose flour

½ tsp salt

Bowl # 2: Milk Wash

3 eggs, beaten

⅓ cup milk

Freshly cracked pepper

Bowl # 3: Seasoned Breadcrumbs

¾ cup (GF) breadcrumbs

½ cup grated Parmesan cheese

⅓ cup fresh Italian parsley after chopping it fine

½ tbsp garlic powder

½ tbsp ground oregano

¼ tsp salt

Freshly cracked pepper

3 tbsp regular olive oil for each pan of cutlets cooked, and more to drizzle into pan as needed so cutlets are not sticking

Pasta sauce (my recipe or a quality jarred sauce)

Grated mozzarella cheese as needed for topping

Fresh basil (optional)

Directions

Dip each piece into the flour.

Then dip into the egg wash.

Then dip into the breadcrumb mixture.

Repeat with each piece until all are breaded.

In a large non-stick frying pan, add olive oil and set heat at medium-high. When the oil is hot but not smoking, gently place meat or eggplant into pan without crowding. Allow to cook while gently shaking pan, and only turn the pieces over when the breading has cooked enough to adhere without falling off. When removing a cooked piece and adding in a new piece to cook, drizzle in more oil as you go along.

Remove from pan when breading is golden brown (chicken may take a little longer to cook). Set on a bake sheet lined with paper towel.

To assemble:

In a large casserole dish, cover the bottom in a thin layer of pasta sauce. Place the pieces on top of the sauce without stacking or crowding.

Spoon about 1 tbsp of pasta sauce on top of each piece, without drowning them.

Spread desired amount of grated mozzarella cheese over each piece.

Drizzle entire pan with a sprinkling of olive oil.

Bake uncovered in a preheated oven at 375°F until cheese is bubbly and getting golden. Top with chopped fresh basil if using. I love to use a large platter in the center of the table for serving. Heat the remainder of the pasta sauce to serve.

<u>Spicy Summer Cannellini Beans & Sausage</u>

I often serve these beans in a dish along with garlic-stuffed olives, an assortment of cheeses, and baguettes or crostini slices. A good GF option for replacing the bread is using my Queijo recipe for pizza dough, simply brushed with olive oil, sprinkled with Parmesan cheese and rosemary, and then baked. You can adjust the amount of beans used, depending on how big a batch you need.

Ingredients

2 cups dry cannellini beans

4 hot Italian sausages (good quality that's laced with lots of anise, is best). A healthier version is using lean chicken, or turkey sausage, but my preference is to use the real thing.

2 tbsp regular olive oil

½ onion, minced

3 garlic cloves, minced

½ cup red wine

1 cup chicken broth

1 can of San Marzano tomatoes diced or pureed

½ tsp crushed chili peppers, or to suit taste

½ tbsp dried basil

½ tbsp dried oregano

1 tsp rosemary

Freshly cracked pepper

Freshly chopped basil for topping

Freshly grated Parmigiano Reggiano for topping

Directions

Preheat oven to 325°.

In a Dutch Oven, cook sausages on the stovetop until they're well seared and almost cooked through. Remove from the pan, slice into thin rounds and set aside.

Spoon off any excess sausage fat from the pot, leaving the crispy bits.

Add the olive oil and onions, and sauté for about two minutes on medium-high heat until onions are translucent. Add the garlic and wine, and simmer for a couple of minutes. Add the broth, tomatoes, crushed chili peppers, herbs, sausage and beans. Season with pepper.

Transfer the pot to an oven. Check the pot in about an hour, and turn the temperature down if they're simmering too hard. If the mixture is too dry, add more broth, and if it's too soupy in consistency, tilt the lid. When the beans are fork tender and the mixture has thickened, they're ready. Top with freshly chopped basil and Parmigiano Reggiano before serving.

Note: Almost all beans call for overnight soaking. If not presoaked, they will take longer to cook, but they'll be just fine.

⁓

<u>My Alternative Pasta Sauce</u>

This recipe is a family favourite. I rarely make it the same way twice, but oddly enough, depending on what's on hand, they fall in love with every incarnation. The premise is simple; don't be afraid to play with it. You can add other vegetables, or, omit what you don't like. The addition of hot Italian sausages works well. It's all a matter of personal preference.

Ingredients

3 tbsp olive oil, or more if needed

4 boneless skinless chicken breasts

1 cup Vidalia or sweet onion – sliced thin

½ cup Kalamata olives – sliced

¼ cup sundried tomatoes — diced

3 garlic cloves, minced

8 button mushrooms, or anything more exotic on hand, sliced – about 1 cup

1 cup white wine

¾ cup 18% cream, warm or room temperature

3 cups chicken broth, or more as needed

1 tbsp (GF) chicken concentrate

½ tsp dried basil

½ tbsp dried oregano

½ tsp crushed chilies, or more to taste

1 zucchini, chopped in quite small pieces

12 extra-large black tiger shrimp – uncooked

Fresh baby spinach, a handful for each plate (optional)

Freshly grated Parmigiano Reggiano, optional

Salt, as desired

Freshly cracked pepper

Linguini or Fettuccini (GF) pasta, cooked al dente

Directions

In a large Dutch Oven, heat olive oil over medium-high heat and sear the chicken, seasoned with a little salt, and cracked pepper, until it's nicely browned. Remove, cool and slice into thick pieces.

Add a little bit more olive oil if necessary, and then add the onion, Kalamata olives, sundried tomatoes, garlic cloves, and mushrooms.

Sauté for about five minutes, or until the mushrooms have rendered their juice and are starting to brown.

Add the wine and reduce for about 10 minutes. Add the cream (since the cream is high enough in fat content it shouldn't separate, but whisking will blend things nicely).

Add the chicken broth and chicken concentrate. Add the seasoning, and more cracked pepper.

Add the chicken and continue to simmer gently uncovered until it reduces to desired thickness — about 1 hour.

About 15 minutes before serving, add the zucchini. About 10 minutes before serving add the shrimp. Top with a little more chicken broth if needed.

Place a handful of fresh spinach on the bottom of each plate (optional). Spoon pasta onto spinach if using, ladle pasta sauce over.

Top with grated Parmigiano Reggiano (optional)

Anyone passionate enough to write about food and diet will appreciate this succinct observation by Andy Rooney of 60 Minutes fame: "The two biggest sellers in bookstores are the cookbooks and the diet books. The cookbooks tell you how to prepare the food and the diet books tell you how not to eat any of it."

V.8

"Obstacles are those frightful things you see when you take your eyes off your goal."

~Henry Ford

The decision to relocate was dropped, without notice, like a bombshell. My parents had decided to leave behind, in my dad's now familiar words, the "rat race" of big city life in Toronto, and relocate to the small northern Ontario city of North Bay, located about twenty minutes away from Mother's hometown of Sturgeon Falls. Dad was going to take a monumental risk and establish a new business, and Mother knew she'd secure secretarial work in a town with government agencies. The enormity of the decision was akin to moving the Mount Rushmore Sculptures to Moscow. My shock was understandable because my parents' lives had always centred around adherence to the familiar, and now, inexplicably, they were embracing this drastic change. I'd always thought they'd swallowed magnets and would forever be attracted to their chairs at the kitchen table on Northcliffe Boulevard.

For me, wondering where my life was headed once the door was locked for the last time was more frightening a notion than seeing ghosts, as none had yet to yank the blankets off my bed on a blustery winter night, and I guess you could say we'd managed to co-exist. Maybe they'd been lovingly watching over me the entire time and would follow me on my way out the door.

As it turned out, the earth didn't crack when we drove out of the neighbourhood on a rainy, dreary autumn after-noon, but there was nevertheless a chasm, and it was painful knowing there was no going back. And what details of my memories would fade first — the stinky snails at the corner grocery store, the taste of freshly made Spumoni gelato, the anticipation of Aunt Hazel's tea biscuits, or the heart-thumping pang of joy when a plate of rigatoni in a simple pasta sauce was set before me?

In the absence of any type of life coaching offered by my parents or whispered in dreams by friendly ghosts, and with a pretty good inkling no sweet signora would be awaiting my arrival, a new reason for insecurity was added to my list.

Denise was adjusting to her new surroundings, but I couldn't find one good reason for thinking serendipity had played a role in any of it. But, there seemed to be a kernel of truth to the notion that when one door closes, another one opens, when my dad dropped me off, at fourteen years old, on the south shore of Lake Nipissing for my official first job at a lodge, where the owners would board me until fall.

The lodge experience proved to be life-altering, my coming of age; wine would no longer be served in Signora's miniature juice glass, each and every "adult" experience being the first. I'd have to rely on being aware, instinctively, of the pitfalls in this strange new world. If my cradle were left alone, not rocked or robbed, this would be a chance to prove myself – to someone, for something.

It wasn't Signora's, but standing in the glorious kitchen of the rustic lodge brought a sense of being *home* with her.

The hardworking elderly owners of European descent had built a successful business and were experienced in dealing with young females hired and boarded for summer employment. Years away from legal drinking age and under their watchful eye, we still managed to sneak out to taverns or mingle discreetly with their guests, but we knew what line to never cross if we wanted to stay until school started. No calls or visits came from my parents, yet there was no twinge of loneliness or desire to leave the most beautiful place on earth to check in with them.

Some mornings, my wonderful new friend Cyndy (whom I lovingly nicknamed Lambchop because she reminded me of ventriloquist Shari Lewis's puppet) and I entered the kitchen with uniforms still damp from being washed in the lake (not tending to them soon enough to properly dry). Although freezing cold, our heads full of cobwebs and painfully tired, we were never a minute late, obediently following instructions to the letter and more than happy to comply. Deep down, the discipline the lady owner required was appreciated, and it propelled me to work my ass off, hoping to be proven worthy of the opportunity provided.

When I returned to the lodge the following summer, it was heartbreaking to learn that the previous owners had retired and the place had been taken over by a couple of big city banker types. Though these foolish misfits were quite close to their own retirement, and presumably experienced in business, they had somehow retained more than their fair share of naiveté, which would lead to the clash of their pipe-dream with reality, in a Big Bang theory sort of way.

They were in over their heads managing the lodge and having trouble with the simplest of tasks, like finding a suitable chef, stocking bait, or making ice. Their sons must have come to them late in life because they honestly looked more like haggard grandparents. The stress of handling the business and tending to their four sons' basic needs proved too much, and it was little wonder they became quite unruly. Before long, the novelty wore off, of having to bathe in the lake or scrounge for leftover food from the kitchen after the guests' needs had taken priority, and I couldn't help but feel sorry for them. A waterfront lodge may look like the most idyllic place on earth, but it doesn't run itself, and the boys got lost in the chaos.

The days of being told, "Idle hands make for no good" — the mantra repeated by the previous owner while we peeled one fifty-pound bag of potatoes after another – was now just a faint echo. We knew more about running the lodge than the new proprietors, and we certainly didn't think we needed rules. A rude awakening contradicting this notion was the night the owner, appearing to be liquored up, had a shotgun in his hand waiting for our return.

The constant need for a replacement chef brought a long line of smooth talking, so-called professionals, all with impeccable résumés supporting their red seal or five-star cooking credentials. In succession, each one would crash and burn from the nightly carousing and get banished from the lodge. Within weeks, the arsenal of chefs-in-waiting was now depleted, and the exhausted owners would have to make do with their last choice, no doubt pickings from the bottom of the barrel.

The cottages were filled with mostly American guests, who had long holidayed at the lodge as a yearly tradition, but the writing was on the wall, and this summer would prove to be the last for many of them. For years, they'd been treated to fare fit for royalty. The large ovens in the back kitchen of the main lodge churned out unsurpassed meals: meats, potatoes, and vegetables you'd devour even if you normally shunned them, bread and buns from hand-kneaded dough, desserts, soups, and casseroles, prepared daily from scratch before dawn. The lake was teeming with pickerel, the homey dining room was surrounded with windows facing dockside, guests had their own private lakeside cottages, and until now they'd all lamented the dreaded end of their holiday. Despite its unfortunate decline, I'll always dream of the place, because it's where, due to sheer good fortune, I met Claude, who happened to drop by with a friend to pick up Lambchop.

Even though the magic evaporated under the new owner-ship, I loved the place and know that Lambchop did too. That second summer we doubled our efforts to smooth things over while serving slop cooked by a clone from Mel's Diner, and if you were looking for something homemade with love, you'd have better luck catching an elusive Muskie. Things were bad enough, but when the precocious chef stopped showing up because of *too many pops* the night before, we knew we had a huge problem. Each morning, fishermen expecting to be on the lake before sunup needed shore lunches, and the other soon-to-arrive guests were expecting to be served whatever their hearts desired for breakfast. The owners were nowhere to be found, though we suspected they were tucked away in their private quarters, no doubt despondent and hungover themselves and, dare I say, would have made matters much worse by their presence.

On the first of these occasions, Lambchop and I and a couple of the other girls tried to avoid panicking, not because we had the situation under control, but there just wasn't time to discuss who got the highest marks in grade eight Home Economics class. I still marvel today at how we managed to light the bank of commercial gas stoves without blowing the lodge to smithereens. For Pete's sake, none of us had ever made breakfast for two, let alone for a packed-to-capacity dining room full of paying guests.

It's hilarious to think those picky guests were ordering entrees even a seasoned chef would've had trouble keeping straight: eggs sunny side up, but yolks not too runny; poached egg on double toasted unbuttered whole wheat bread with a side of crispy bacon; fried egg white omelet with double old cheddar, hold the peppers; hot Red River cereal, not too thick but not too runny; and so the list went on. We did stellar work overall and more than deserved to pat ourselves on the back. As for the diners' reactions, let's just say most of what they could identify on their plates was eaten, and they were all the richer by hanging onto their tip money.

Keeping things streamlined, with the goal of learning from each mistake, was key to keeping the whole lot of guests from staging a mutiny. It also worked wonders teaching me how good it feels to reap the reward of staying the course.

While I was finding my footing, Dad too, was finding his as he toiled away in his new workshop located in the rear of an old commercial building near the downtown core. Any happiness he felt by following his dream, that of transforming his home-based business into a full-time venture, was tempered with growing discontent. Scientific glassblowing might have been his passion, but unfortunately, designing and creating neon signs that paid the bills with a full-time job in Toronto would haunt his existence here for the same reason.

Ironically, within a few short years of relocating, he was diagnosed with cancer, the treatment for which was unavailable in North Bay. It was heart-wrenching to see him forced to make the tiring, long treks back to the "rat race" of Toronto, the city he had just escaped from and had vowed he'd never miss seeing again.

Following Dad's death, change seemed to occur at lightning speed. Denise married and moved to Ottawa, and Mother asked if I'd mind her leaving me to move to another province. The fact that she was getting remarried wasn't as shocking as the identity of her groom: her first cousin. It wasn't actually all that unseemly — they hadn't laid eyes on each other since childhood and, after he showed up and aggressively pursued her, she opted for companionship. With my disconnect to her, any discipline was self-taught anyway, so why not be, in my late teens, the queen of my own castle?

Unlike our Queen, however, I had no servants, no fortune, and no corgi as of yet, and the need to be frugal was always forefront in my mind. It helped when a couple of girlfriends moved in and chipped-in on the rent from money earned with part-time jobs. We also took on superintendent duties in the building and managed to eke by financially.

There was, however, still a desire to supplement my meager income, which led to applying for a job as a part-time bartender. My qualifications as a mixologist were about on par with being a building superintendent — extending no further than having used a beer bottle opener and figuring out how to empty the canister on a vacuum. In other words, I didn't have any. A quick review of a bartender's manual would have to do the trick. After all, how difficult could it be to mix a few drinks?

All in all, things went pretty well. The owner of the restaurant didn't fire me for the countless mistakes, like omitting the orange juice in Singapore Slings, and the birthday boy survived having a whole tray of Shirley Temple drinks dumped on him when I tried to impress the table with my one-handed tray-carrying skills. The kid's mother was huffing about, but, honestly, could she not appreciate that, per my highly developed awareness of social etiquette, I was attempting to serve the birthday boy first?

With my part-time career change from bartender to dining room waitress well underway (a dicey move on the manager's part given that my likely forte was dish washing), any precious time off was spent revelling in the joy of cooking for myself. With my first Thanksgiving turkey, the *surprise* bag of gizzards appeared during the carving portion of my inspired presentation. At no point would my love of cooking assist in helping me become a chef of any sort. To this day, I'm clueless as to whether you would baste Foie Gras, or tar and feather it. My apron is always on by mid-afternoon, and unless there's a special occasion, everyday cooking is fresh and simple, just as it should be.

Never having to answer to a bloody soul, and playing house grownup style, suited me just fine, but I knew, intuitively, that the teenage years might come up a little short of groovy. It turns out though, even with various obstacles that couldn't be ignored, I strived, with little direction, to achieve a higher goal (wisely using my personal yardstick to measure the distance, which is all that matters) than simply eking by, and the effort eventually paid off.

Most memories are crammed into a well-sealed pot in a mind pantry, and it can startle me when one pops up out of the blue. There are, however, a few precious ones that are always simmering, without a lid, on the surface of my subconscious being — shards of glass, and neon light.

V.9

"Donna modesta famiglia onesta." (Modest woman, honest family.)

~Italian folklore

Although still in my teens, it seemed to be the right time to tie the knot. Marrying Claude would please Mother. From the moment she first laid eyes on him she'd determined he'd make a fine husband, and she did have impeccable taste.

A summer wedding was out of the question. My internal thermostat has never worked, and my face is what sweats the most, especially when I'm flustered or nervous. As a matter of comfort, and a practicality worthy of Mother, we decided the simple exchange of vows should be tucked into part of the Christmas season celebrations. We spoke to the priest and he agreed to sanctify the marriage with nothing other than a short, private, blessing which would follow the scheduled afternoon baptisms. The date was set for December 24, 1979.

A charming, two-piece off-white outfit was purchased, and apart from making dinner reservations, we were ready to call the parents to advise them of our plan.

The phone call to Mother fell flat. After announcing that no daughter of hers was going to look like she needed a shotgun wedding (which definitely wasn't the case), she abruptly decided to take matters into her own hands. Voilà, within the wink of an eye we now had an official wedding planner. Let that sink in. Mother. The. Wedding. Planner. Perhaps she'd received an etiquette manual from the Queen's Lady in Waiting to guide her? Who the hell knows!

We barely survived. The ceremony was held at Paroisse Saint-Vincent-de-Paul, an impressive landmark that has one of the largest congregational seating capacities in our small city. A full-scale Catholic wedding can be a lengthy affair, which is fine, but I didn't understand a word spoken during the entire French service. At least the guests, which numbered a mere ninety-four, didn't complain about needing extra elbowroom.

As I walked down the aisle in a nervous sweat, bedecked in a fur-trimmed satiny confection, donning a pearly skullcap (think turn-of-the-century beanie cap worn to bed on a cold prairie night), my eyes came upon the pale, stone-like groom. He was donning the best man's boutonniere instead of his own, and sure didn't appear ready to greet his blushing bride. It seemed painfully obvious that he'd suffered some sort of trauma, cold feet perhaps, and I wondered whether his parents cemented him into position after drugging and hog-tying him for transportation.

As the evening wore down, we headed to our room and ordered a magnificent pizza with double cheese and pepperoni, devouring it while Mother and her guests waltzed about in the reception room. After an exciting day peppered with rosy proclamations, and anxiously anticipating the morning introduction to married life, Italian food was, nostalgically, an appropriate bedtime feast.

It's striking how things go. When Mother hijacked the wedding plans, the date of our wedding was changed to December 21st, which is the winter solstice, the longest night and the shortest day of the year. Mother Nature allows her creations to fittingly rest during this season, with the joyful promise of renewal when spring arrives.

"Wedding Day" Dec. 21, 1979

It wasn't revealed until after we were married that Claude, as a scrappy little kid, had sat alone on a large boulder on the family farm and promised himself that he'd be in control of his own destiny. His thoughts must have been in technicolor because our exciting ride on a carpet crafted with durable thread has been pretty awesome.

In 1985, and in the spirit of this vow, we took a chance and became self-employed. Claude set aside his work as a skilled, licensed tradesman, I abandoned my real estate license, and with nothing more than a pocketful of good intentions, a kiss for luck, and countless Hail Marys on my part, we bought Ivan's Restaurant (A North Bay Tradition), initially established as Ted's Snack Bar in 1945.

My memories are vivid of being in Sturgeon Falls in the '60s, and anxiously anticipating our mandatory trip to Ted's in North Bay. At the time, it was located in a small shed-like building (long ago torn down) with a walk-up counter. There were large pots on a back stove filled with fresh cobs of corn, and the wieners on a stick needed for Ted's famous Pronto Pups (corndogs) were dipped in batter per order and then fried to a golden crisp. Fresh-cut fries slathered in Ted's homemade gravy completed the feast. It seemed surreal that we were now at the helm of a traditional landmark that had long ago become part of the community's fabric.

From the start, ownership suited us perfectly, and we thrived with having the benefit of tried and true recipes and a great staff, which meant that neither of us had to be the chief cook and bottle washer.

We'd stay on top of new products and trends by escaping whenever possible to traipse through all sorts of trade shows. We entered that first one in a state of awe – the showroom had to be the size of two football fields combined! It was shocking — like peering into a frosty store window at Christmas and *Mother* telling me she'd pre-purchased all the poodle puppies for my gift.

Forget about dancing sugarplums! The array of platters stacked with assorted bite-sized concoctions was mind-boggling, and I easily succumbed to the allure of the inviting toothpicks stuck in sample meatballs. The thought of how much food must be wasted during the show weighed on my mind, but after a quick look at the size of my purse, it became a simple matter of enjoying what could be swallowed on site.

With the restaurant open seven days a week, it wasn't easy to get away, but we'd never miss making the trip during the holiday season to see Mother, who now resided in Ste. Cecile de Masham, Quebec.

We'd have to travel through Parc de la Gatineau (Quebec's Outaouais region), which meant a desolate trek once the sun went down. Apart from animal tracks, the deep white snow looked like Mother Nature herself had personally arranged each flake to make sure the canvas for her Christmas card appeared smooth. If the moon was full, its proximity seemed too close to the trees, outlandishly large and far too bright – like a celestial ornament to light the way. I marvelled at the enormous, stark black trees, drawn into the surreal scene using ink from a dipping well; the frozen patches of trunk mould, pale green and creamy, painted in thick acrylic; and the charcoal penciled evergreen trees, feather-edged by fingertip.

The journey may have been serenely mystical, but it was also foreboding. Never mind the possibility of the car breaking down — any misstep navigating the hilly and icy dirt road could cause it to careen off course and land us in the ditch. And back in the day, the only person with a cell phone was Inspector Gadget.

In the early years we'd make the trip in a Volkswagen Beetle. Guaranteed, a woman didn't design the heating system in the contraption! Being a nervous co-pilot, with a tendency to swear like a drunken sailor, I think Claude probably wanted to tie me to the roof, but he needed me to continually scrape ice from the *interior* windshield. The pipe delivering the heat was precisely directed at his crotch, which meant the only appropriate carol to sing was "Chestnuts Roasting on an Open Fire." Once the kids were in the picture, we were driving a hatchback, and although it was warmer, you couldn't find them after they were strapped into their seats, layers of cozy quilts using the Russian technique for assembling Matryoshka nesting dolls keeping them warm.

Claude and I ran the restaurant for over two decades, and, in addition to countless happy memories, it deserves credit for playing an important role in my gastronomic journey. When the time came to direct more of our focus on commercial real estate holdings, our daughter Kristina decided to take on a challenge, which would upend her life out west. She'd ultimately put a business degree to good use by returning to purchase the restaurant, and we're proud to say that, under her keenly astute stewardship, the tradition continues. The time-honoured recipes (I miss them all dearly), or methods of cooking, haven't changed much since 1945, some, not at all. If it's not broken, don't fix it!

Throughout the years, I've run like a chicken and twirled like a top with the best of them, while having the appreciation of what the essence of tradition means. The definition of tradition according to Google Dictionary is *"the transmission of customs or beliefs from generation to generation, or the fact of being passed on in this way."* It's not always possible for a family to set a tradition for everyday living due to life's constraints, but it's important to be mindful of the meaning.

Traditions

> *"Maybe the cat has fallen into the stew, or the lettuce has frozen, or the cake has collapsed. Eh bien, tant pis. Usually one's cooking is better than one thinks it is. And if the food is truly vile, then the cook must simply grit her teeth and bear it with a smile and learn from her mistakes."*
>
> *~ Julia Child*

I'm happy to share recipes that are part of *my* tradition. I was hellbent on creating some sort of thread connecting each holiday, and I didn't care if it meant serving Yorkshire pudding — a traditional accompaniment to roast beef — with turkey at Thanksgiving, which I still do because the kids love it.

One cherished thread, in particular, links the past to the present and it belongs to my beloved late mother-in-law Mathilda (referred to as Mémère). She always carried herself with a dignified classiness brought forward from an era where being ladylike wasn't an option; it was an art form. Having raised ten children, she knew what real hardship looked like, working as a modern woman outside the home, yet running a farm consisting of hundreds of acres. Luckily, she passed down family recipes, which were explained to me verbally over the years, and I've been able to recreate them with the help of Claude's sisters Diane and Annette. I am forever grateful for their guidance, because these recipes mean the world to all of us.

The Ledoux forefathers initially came from France, and, while I believe the recipes survived in spirit, they did evolve and become uniquely Canadian as they were passed down from one generation to another. There'll be some authenticity to true French cuisine, but there will also be a regional flair, and then a familial flair, and then a little of my own flair.

Without the Ledoux recipes I've carried forward and cherish, Christmas wouldn't be worth taking out of the box. The foods have distinct flavours that give them their seasonal or Christmas designation, and they're only eaten during the holiday season, which makes them special.

Below is Mémère's timetable that she followed for serving each of the dishes, which would be typical of most French-Canadian families, and, yes, she made two Sea Pies.

Mémère's Christmas Holiday Serving Guide

Christmas Eve

Tourtière (Meat Pie); Baked Ham; Cold Meat Platter including her reserved Roast Beef used for making the Ragout; Humble Christmas Salad; Potato and Macaroni Salads; Cheese and Pickle Tray; Buns; trays of homemade baked goods including Pets de Soeur (Nuns Farts, which I have no recipe for, but you can google it), and Butter Tarts.

Christmas Day

Sea Pie; Turkey and Gravy; Mashed Potatoes; Turnip; Corn; Humble Christmas Salad; Cheese and Pickle Tray; Buns; sweet tray as noted above.

New Year's Day

Sea Pie; Ragout; Tourtière; Mashed Potatoes; Humble Christmas Salad; Cheese and Pickle Tray; Buns; Sweet Tray as noted above.

<u>Sea Pie – Cipaille</u>

Chef Andrew Bridgman has graciously provided me with the following explanation for Sea Pie, which is part of his research collection on regional cooking in Canada.

"Sea Pie, Cipaille or Cipate can be traced back to the English, the French and Canadian native tribes located in the Northeast.

The earliest accounts suggest the English in the French province of Quebec introduced the pie, and the wives of sailors who were heading out on voyages made it. The 'Sea' Pie was not made with fish or seafood, but rather with game meats. The sailors would have their fill of fish and seafood and meats were a welcome variation out at sea.

There is evidence that the French adopted the pie and renamed it phonetically to Cipaille. It later became known as Cipate in some regions of Quebec. The pie was similarly made with game meats with the exception of the Gaspe (Quebec region), who made their Cipate with salmon. In Quebec Cipaille and Cipate are considered a part of the province's culinary culture.

The Montagnais tribe of Saguenay-Lac-St. Jean always considered a Cipaille of game meats their festive dish. They also considered layered desserts with berries to be a Cipaille as well. The biggest variation of Cipaille for the northeastern natives was they generally made theirs in clay pots. They covered the pots with dough made from wheat supplied by settlers."

As for the seasoning of this dish, a combination of ground cinnamon and cloves is used. If you're not accustomed to using these spices, you might want to fry a few cubes of meat in a small pan and add a tiny pinch of the seasoning for a taste test. We love the dish because of the distinct flavour, but like anything else, it might be an acquired taste for some. Some recipes for Sea Pie use allspice instead of cloves and cinnamon, but I wouldn't think of changing my recipe. The wondrous aroma of Christmas cooking that escapes into the frigid air from an open door will waken bears out of hibernation.

I prepare my meat a day ahead as a matter of convenience. If you do so, bring the meat to room temperature before assembly.

To give you an idea of the size of pot you'll need, my large Dutch Oven is a Staub 7qt cast iron pot.

Ingredients for Meat Mixture

Never use meat that has previously been frozen. It must be fresh.

2½ lbs beef, cubed into ½ inch pieces (The meat will tenderize but ask the butcher for a good cut.)

2½ lbs pork roast, cubed into ½ inch pieces

1 lb boneless, skinless chicken breasts, cubed into ½-inch pieces

2 tsp jarred organic garlic puree (optional)

Ground pepper

½ tsp salt

Ground cloves, to taste

Ground cinnamon, to taste

4-5 cooking onions, thinly sliced to make rings — not minced or diced

Chicken broth, as much as needed (I never let my stock of broth get depleted)

Ingredients for Dough

2 eggs

1¼ cup milk

(GF) Flour – 2½ cups to start and more as needed to gather dough into ball

2 tsp baking soda

¾ tsp salt

¼ cup lard – chilled in fridge before using for at least 30 minutes

Directions

Add 2 eggs to a measuring cup and fork beat. Add milk to bring it to the 1¼ cup measure. Set aside.

In a large mixing bowl, add flour, baking soda, and salt. Stir. Add lard and incorporate using a pastry blender or 2 knives, until you've got a nice crumble.

Add egg and milk mixture to dry ingredients. Using your hands or a silicone spatula, mix while gathering everything into a ball.

Sprinkle a generous amount of flour onto your working surface. Set the dough onto the flour, and using your hands, continue gathering and folding, adding a little flour if needed, until you have a smooth ball. Wrap the dough in cling wrap and set aside.

Note: My mother-in-law always used regular flour and she didn't chill her dough before rolling it out when making this particular dish.

Assembly

Preheat oven to 350°

Cut the beef, pork and chicken as evenly as possible into ½-inch cubes. Season well with freshly cracked pepper and salt. Add garlic if using. Garlic doesn't appear to be included in traditional sea pie, but I always add it. With your hands, mix the meats to blend together well. You will only add the cloves and cinnamon during the assembly.

Pour about an inch (roughly ¾ cup) of chicken stock in the bottom of the Dutch Oven. Place the first layer of meat, approximately two inches in thickness (roughly 3 cups), in the bottom. Separate each sliced onion round into rings to cover (roughly 1½ small cooking onions per layer).

Sprinkle the layer lightly with cinnamon and cloves. Season with ground cracked pepper and a very small pinch of salt.

Divide your dough into 3 sections. Roll out your first ball, making sure that it's large enough to cover. Set the dough over the onions and gently press into place.

Set the next layer of meat, onions and seasoning, and cover with dough. Repeat, for the final layer, using the last piece of dough to cover. Make a small steam hole in the center.

Trickle chicken broth down the outer edge of the dough all the way around the pot (roughly ¾ cup broth), and a little into the steam hole. Do not pour any liquid over the top layer of dough.

Place the covered pot in the oven for one hour. Then turn the oven temperature down to 225°F, and continue baking for at least 4 hours. Check the pot at the 3-hour mark and if you're not seeing any bubbling liquid you can add a bit more broth down the sides.

<u>Ledoux Ragout - Pork Meatballs in Gravy</u>

For the Christmas feasts, Mémère would start preparing days ahead. For this ragout, she'd brown her flour, roast a beef, roast a pork, and bake a chicken, preserving the broths from the meats to combine together. The beef, once cooked, is not used in the assembly of the ragout, but put away to be served on the meat platter as part of the feast, or used for sandwiches (fabulous with my homemade mayo recipe).

Christmas wouldn't be the same without this dish, and any effort it takes to prepare it is more than worthwhile.

It's easier to cook the beef and pork roast together to save time, if you have a large enough cooking vessel. I use my Staub 7qt. Dutch Oven.

Ingredients

Note for shopping: 1 liter or quart of chicken broth is roughly 4 cups

1 beef roast (about 2½ lbs)

1 pork picnic shoulder, bone in (about 3½ lbs)

1 roasting chicken (about 4 lbs)

1 cooking onion roughly chopped

5 cups of chicken broth for beef and pork

3 cups of chicken broth for chicken

Cracked pepper to taste

1 cup browned flour (see method under "Browned Flour for Gravy")

8 more cups of chicken broth to be added later (You might not need all of it, but have it on hand)

Ingredients for Meatballs

4 lbs ground pork, lean

1 large cooking onion, minced finely

6 garlic cloves, minced finely

1 tbsp ground cloves

¾ tbsp ground cinnamon

1 level tsp salt

Cracked pepper, to taste

Ingredients for Gravy Thickener

½ cup water

4 tbsp (GF) all-purpose browned flour

Freshly cracked pepper

Directions

Preheat oven to 350°F.

Set the roast of beef and pork into large Dutch Oven. Cover with 5 cups of chicken broth. This is a large amount of liquid but the main purpose for cooking these meats is for the broth. Roughly chop the cooking onion into the pot, and then season with cracked pepper.

Set the chicken into its roaster and cover with 3 cups of chicken broth. Season with cracked pepper.

Bake both pots at 350°F for the first hour.

Reduce heat and continue baking both pots at 275°F for 2 hours.

Reduce the heat and continue baking the meats at 225°F for another 1½ hours or so. The chicken can be pulled out sooner if it's falling apart.

Remove meats and pour the broths from both pots into a large stock pot. (You'll need a large one because you'll be adding your meats in later.) Once the liquid has cooled, transfer to fridge for several hours or overnight, so the lardy fat can rise to the top. If you want to make the Ragout in one day, you can add ice cubes to the cooled broth which will attract the lardy fat to be spooned off.

Debone the chicken and refrigerate once cooled. Don't be worrying about breaking up the larger chicken parts into smaller pieces because once it cooks into the ragout it will be completely shredded anyway. The same thing goes with the pork roast. Set aside the beef roast for other uses.

Remove the lardy fat that has risen to the top of the refrigerated broth, and then strain it through a sieve or colander. I'll use another pot that's large enough to contain the broth (you haven't added the meat in yet so a decently good-sized pot will do), and then transfer it back to the large stock pot.

To Make Meatballs:

In a large bowl, mix the pork, onion, garlic, seasonings, and salt and pepper. I use my hands to make sure the spices are evenly distributed.

Roll the meatballs. They shouldn't be overly large – about the size of a cocktail meatball.

Set onto a large pan and generously sprinkle them with the browned flour, shaking the pan to ensure they're well coated. You'll use about a ½ cup of flour for coating. Set aside the remainder of the flour to be used for thickening the gravy before serving.

Return the pot of strained, defatted broth to the stove and set to high heat. Add 4 cups of chicken broth.

Gently set the meatballs into the broth. Once they're all in, add in more chicken broth if needed to ensure they're well covered in liquid. Reduce your heat to medium-low and let them simmer gently for about 30 minutes.

Add the chicken and pork meat into the pot with the meatballs.

Note for freezing: At this point when making them ahead, before adding flour thickener, I divide the meats between three plastic containers (each container can hold 8 cups) and distribute the broth evenly so the meats are well covered in broth, and freeze until ready to use. On the day I'm serving the ragout, I set everything back into my large stockpot and defrost on low heat.

Adjust the liquid level by adding more chicken broth if needed to ensure all the meat is well covered, and season with cracked pepper. Bring the pot to a gentle boil and thicken to make gravy to desired consistency (see directions below), then reduce the heat to low and cover until serving. You may not require a lot of additional thickening because the gravy will already be somewhat thick from the flour on the meatballs.

Directions for Gravy Thickener

Add the cold water to a glass jar with a tight-fitting lid.

Add the (GF) flour and shake thoroughly. Make certain when you remove the lid that any flour that falls from the lid is pushed down into the liquid. If you see little clumps or balls of flour, smooth out with a fork before shaking again.

Once the mixture is the right consistency you can slowly drizzle a few drops into your boiling broth while whisking constantly. Watch to see if it blends in. If you see it forming little balls of goo, your mixture is too thick so add more water. If all is well, continue slowly drizzling in until desired thickness.

Tourtière - Meat Pie

Tourtière is a French-Canadian dish that's often served during the traditional Réveillon, which is a nighttime feast on Christmas Eve.

In Lower Canada, which is now the province of Quebec, the dish was made in coastal areas with fish, most commonly salmon, and in inland areas, with beef, pork, or veal, or a combination thereof. It's also a traditional Christmas dish for towns in American states that straddle the Canadian border, notably Maine, Rhode Island, Vermont, New Hampshire and Massachusetts.

There's no best recipe for this pie. Families that have the tradition of making it will fiercely pronounce their recipe as best, and balk if you dare put forth something that veers from what they consider perfection. I'm married to a Frenchman, and most of his siblings have married into French families, and you'd be surprised at how many recipe variations I've been exposed to.

Madame Benoît, who hailed from Quebec, was a renowned Canadian chef, culinary author, and speaker who trained at both the Sorbonne and Cordon Bleu cooking schools in Paris. In her recipe, cloves are cited as a necessity for a truly authentic Quebec dish. In the Ledoux family, cloves and cinnamon are both used, and in my recipe version, I'm not as conservative as some with the seasoning.

The addition of breadcrumbs is the more common addition to the meat mixture to absorb excess fat, but over the years I've tried variations, using grated raw potatoes or mashed potatoes. The addition of mashed potatoes suits me best.

Ingredients

I use about 6 pounds of meat and get three good-sized pies. You can use just pork, but I don't consider using just beef an option. If you're using the GF pie dough recipe that I've included, you'll need to make three batches. It's best to make one batch of dough at a time (one bottom and one top), instead of attempting to triple the dough recipe.

4 lbs lean ground pork

2 lbs lean ground beef

2 medium cooking onions, finely chopped

3 large garlic cloves, crushed and minced finely

1 tsp celery salt

Freshly cracked pepper to taste

1½ tbsp ground cloves, or more to taste

¾ tbsp ground cinnamon, or more to taste

Salt if needed (optional)

2 lbs of potatoes, cooked with 1 tsp salt, and mashed – about 6 potatoes

Traditionalists might flip, but I add a few dashes of hot sauce (Franks's Red Hot) to wake things up when the meat is simmering, which, of course, is optional. Many recipes also omit garlic, but I prefer to add it. It's more a nod to a little spiciness, and my own flair.

GF Pie Crusts, recipe to follow. The shells for meat pie are not parbaked.

Directions

Set stove to medium heat. In a large stock pot mix the meats, add the onion, garlic, celery salt and cracked pepper. Add a few dashes of hot sauce if using. Adjust your heat to a simmer.

As the meat is simmering add the ground cloves and cinnamon. Once the meat is cooked and still on the heat, I taste and readjust the seasoning using a ½ tsp at a time of each spice until I'm happy with the spice balance. This is when I'll season with a little salt if needed. I do not drain off the fat, but if the liquid is excessive and the meat is too submerged, ladle a little off the top.

Remove from heat and add in two cups of mashed potatoes. Let stand for ten minutes. The mixture should be thick enough but still a bit saucy, so keep adding the remaining mashed potatoes,1 cup at a time (you'll likely be using them all), to get this consistency.

Line up your unbaked GF pie shells. Stir the meat between scooping it into the shells, so each pie will have the same consistency. Cover with top shell, seal the edges and pierce holes in it with a fork. Some cooks will brush the top with milk or melted butter.

Bake pies at 350°F until they are golden brown. Let cool. The pies will freeze nicely.

GF Pie Crust

Finding Nicole Hunn's website "Gluten Free on a Shoestring" was a blessing! Her blog is wonderful, and her Extra Flaky Gluten Free Pie Crust is a game-changer. It's simple to make and the dough rolls out beautifully. I wanted to cry when I was able to use my rolling pin again because the dough was actually pliable.

Nicole is far more adept at using a rolling pin, so I've slightly altered her instructions to more accurately reflect the method that works for me. To see her exact recipe or a short video of her making the dough, visit: glutenfreeonashoestring.com.

One batch of dough will give you one bottom shell and one top shell.

Ingredients

1½ cups (210 g) all-purpose GF flour, plus more for sprinkling

¾ tsp xanthan gum (omit if your flour blend already contains it)

¼ tsp baking powder

½ tsp kosher salt (I used regular)

6 tbsp (84 g) unsalted butter, roughly chopped and chilled

½ cup (120 g) sour cream (full fat, preferably), chilled

Ice water by the teaspoonful, as necessary

Directions

In a large bowl, place the flour, xanthan gum, baking powder and salt, and whisk to combine well. Add the chopped and chilled butter, and toss to coat it in the dry ingredients. Flatten each chunk of butter between your thumb and forefinger. Add the sour cream, and mix to moisten the dry ingredients. The dough should be shaggy and somewhat crumbly. Knead the dough together with clean hands until it begins to come together. Add ice water by the teaspoon only if necessary, for the dough to hold together. Turn the dough out onto a sheet of plastic wrap, and press into a disk as you close the plastic wrap around the dough. It will still seem rough. Place the dough in the refrigerator to chill for 30 minutes.

Preheat your oven to 375°F. Grease a 9-inch metal pie plate generously and set aside.

Once the dough has chilled, turn it out onto a lightly floured piece of unbleached parchment paper.

Sprinkle the dough lightly with flour, and roll it out, moving the dough frequently and sprinkling it lightly with flour if it begins to stick.

Fold the dough over onto itself like you would a business letter, until it is a rectangle about 1 inch thick.

Sprinkle the dough again lightly with flour, and roll out the dough once again.

Repeat the rolling and folding procedure until the dough becomes pliable.

Cover half the dough in saran wrap and set aside for the top crust.

Roll the other half out into an approximate 12-inch round. Loosely fold it in half and gently center it over half the pie plate, and then unfold the top half to cover the full plate. Lift up the edges of the crust gently to create slack in the crust while placing it into the bottom and up the sides of the pie plate.

After trimming off the excess dough with kitchen shears, tuck the excess pie crust under itself, and crimp the edge gently all the way around the crust by pinching the dough at regular intervals with one hand, and creating a crimped impression with the forefinger of the other hand.

**Cover the pie crust with plastic wrap and place it in the refrigerator to chill until firm, at least 30 minutes (and up to 3 days).*

**Note: I didn't follow the last step (missed it by accident), and instead of refrigerating it, I just put my filling in. The dough was still great.*

Parbaked Crust (If recipe requires par-baking).

Remove the pie crust from the refrigerator and discard the plastic. Pierce the bottom of the pie crust all over with the tines of a fork. Place a sheet of parchment paper on the raw crust and cover with pie weights or dried beans. Place in the center of the preheated oven and bake until the crust is lightly golden brown on the edges, about 10 minutes. Remove the pie weights and parchment and allow the crust to cool before proceeding with your recipe.

Turkey

This will sound ridiculous to most people, but the tradition of dancing with the turkey before it goes into the pan has been passed along to my children. My grandkids always remind me not to forget, but little do they know it's impossible to forgo a trot with a turkey. Once it's washed, and before it's stuffed, I take it by its wings and let its feet dance along the counter, down one way, and back the other. Thoughts of thankfulness, with remembrance for those no longer with us, go along with the dance. Before the turkey goes into the oven it's rubbed down generously with butter, and sprinkled with paprika. Season with salt (including cavity), and cracked pepper.

We often cook the turkey on the Green Egg, a ceramic cooker, derived from the design of ancient clay cookers known as kamado. The unique ceramic composition of the egg (it's actually shaped like one) is fueled by firewood and can handle extremely intense heat and yet gives you exceptional control when smoking meats. It can also be used much like any other type of wood-fired grill, creating meats that are decadently tender. No wonder devoted users are referred to as "Eggheads."

Using the Green Egg, the turkey skin is gloriously crisp, and, when you pierce it with your fork, the juice will sometimes shoot straight across the room.

We're careful about not letting the bird get too smoky-tasting, and set the venting accordingly. If you haven't used this cooking method but are tempted to try it, be mindful of the smoke factor and do a little homework beforehand.

It would be hard to capture turkey drippings to make a gravy, when the turkey is standing upright on a stand in the Green Egg. Therefore, I'll make my gravy ahead by roasting another small turkey a week or so before Christmas (using the meat for soups, et cetera), and then freezing the gravy until needed. Believe it, or not, it sounds like I complicate things, but it's one less chore to worry about on Christmas day.

For traditional oven baking a turkey: According to the Turkey Farmers of Canada guidelines, a properly cooked turkey should be: 180°F in thigh, 170°F in breast, and stuffing must reach a temperature of 165°F. For further information regarding turkey matters go to: www.turkeyfarmersofcanada.ca.

⌒

<u>Gravy for Traditional Oven-Roasted Turkey</u>

Ingredients

Note for shopping: 1 liter or quart of chicken broth is roughly 4 cups

1½ cups water

8 tbsp (GF) Flour

2 pkg (25g paper packet) Turkey Gravy mix (I use GF Club House brand) or ⅓ cup of Bisto if you're not making it GF

10 cups chicken broth – you'll use 8 cups, but may need a good bit more

2 tbsp liquid chicken concentrate

Cracked pepper

Directions

Remove turkey from oven, remove stuffing (recipe to follow) to covered casserole dish, cover turkey with foil, and set both aside to keep warm.

Set roasting pan on stove on medium-high heat. Add 4 cups of chicken broth. Scrape up the bits in the bottom of the pan as it comes to a simmer, and then remove from heat and strain liquid into large Dutch Oven.

To prepare gravy mixture, add the cold water to a glass jar with a tight-fitting lid.

Add the flour and Turkey Gravy mix and shake thoroughly. Make certain when you remove the lid that any flour that falls from the lid is pushed down into the liquid. If you see little clumps or balls of flour, smooth out with a fork before shaking again.

Set cast iron pot on stovetop and turn temperature to high, and then add another 4 cups of chicken broth and cracked pepper. Add chicken concentrate. If you want a larger pot of gravy add more chicken broth, as desired. When liquid comes to a boil start to drizzle in flour mixture. Watch to see if it blends in. If you see it forming little balls of goo, your mixture is too thick so add more water. If all is well, continue slowly drizzling in until desired thickness. Reduce heat to a gentle simmer and cover.

Stuffing

For years, my stuffing was made using my homemade GF bread but, as GF bread has improved in texture, I find it more convenient to use store-bought. Promise brand makes a sliced Brioche GF bread and it's fabulous for stuffing.

Ingredients

1 loaf of homemade bread or 1½ loaves of store-bought as they're smaller in size

½ cup butter (1 foil stick)

4 celery stalks, chopped

2 cooking onions, diced

1½ tbsp dried parsley

2 garlic cloves, minced

1½ tbsp (GF) liquid chicken concentrate or other chicken bouillon

Freshly cracked pepper

2 tbsp sage seasoning, or more

2 tbsp poultry seasoning, or more

2 tsp savory seasoning

Freshly cracked pepper to suit your taste

1½ cups chicken broth, more or less

Directions

Preheat oven to 325°F. Place whole slices of bread on a large stainless-steel tray and set in oven. Bake until bread is dried out (it doesn't have to be browned as it would be if toasted). Turn slices frequently so both sides dry evenly. Remove from oven, cool, and then, using your hands, break the bread into bite-sized pieces (1"x 1") into a very large bowl.

In a large skillet melt butter over medium heat. Add the celery, onion, parsley, garlic, chicken concentrate, and season with pepper. Sauté until onion is translucent and celery is softened.

Pour the contents over the broken pieces of bread (I use a silicone spatula to swipe the skillet clean). Add the seasonings, and then slowly drizzle the chicken broth over the mixture while tossing until all pieces are moistened well but not mushy and the pieces somewhat cling together. Taste and add more seasoning if desired. Stuff the inside of the turkey once it's been carefully washed and salted.

<u>Stuffing Made Outside the Turkey Cavity</u>

When making a dressing separate from the turkey (when turkey is cooked on the Green Egg), I purchase an assortment of turkey thighs and necks (6-8 pieces). If these parts aren't available, use any other parts at the meat counter that are sold to be used for making stock.

Add 2 tbsp olive oil and 2 tbsp margarine into a large Dutch Oven and sear the turkey pieces well on stovetop (about 10 minutes). Season with freshly cracked pepper. Once seared, remove and set aside.

Spoon out excess fat, leaving about a tbsp in the pot, and then pour a little chicken stock into the bottom – about ½ a cup. Spoon in ½ the dressing (as made in my Stuffing recipe), and then set the turkey necks around the outer edge of the dressing to form a cozy little wall. Add the remaining dressing, and cover well with the remainder of the seared turkey parts. Drizzle about ½ cup chicken broth over the turkey parts and season with cracked pepper. Cover and bake in a preheated oven at 325°F for approximately 2 hours. As it's cooking you can add a little more chicken broth down the sides if it's drier than you'd like. Internal temperature should be 165°F.

Grandma Lorna Walkling's Cranberry Sauce

Ingredients

1-12 oz. pkg fresh cranberries

1 cup of water

1 cup sugar

1 tsp orange rind

2 tbsp (1oz.) Grand Marnier, Cognac or Brandy (optional)

Directions

Rinse cranberries. In a small saucepan mix sugar and water and bring to a boil. Add cranberries and boil until their skins pop, about 5 minutes. Reduce heat to simmer and add the orange rind. Add the liqueur if using. Simmer for about 5 minutes. Remove from heat, cool, and refrigerate. This recipe will make about 2 ½ cups.

Nana's Carrots

Yes, my grandkids think they're magical!

Use the amount of carrots desired. Cut them in half lengthwise. If the carrots are thick, cut lengthwise again, so you'll have 2-4 long pieces, per carrot.

In a large deep saucepan on stovetop, cover the carrots in water with ½ tsp salt, bring to a boil, and then simmer until blanched but still quite firm.

Remove carrots from pan, drain water, and set aside until just before dinner.

When ready to finish cooking: Turn the stovetop to medium-high heat and add 1 tbsp olive oil and 2 tbsp butter. Add the carrots to the pan. Season with salt and cracked pepper.

The heat should be high enough that the carrots will start to brown nicely in the butter. Once they're fork tender and golden remove from heat and transfer to serving platter. Sprinkle with freshly minced thyme (if desired) and serve.

Sometimes I'll add 2 tbsp of brandy, cognac, or Grand Marnier before removing the carrots from the pan. Lighting the liqueur to flambé is a bit risky so make sure to have a fire extinguisher handy, especially if you've used a can of hair-spray for your beehive.

⌇

<u>Nana's Mashed Potatoes</u>

Nana, unfortunately, can't bake, but I do make, as per the grandkid's constant requests, lots of mashed potatoes.

*My hands-down favourite liquid for making mashed potatoes is (Carnation) evaporated milk (**not sweetened**) that has been warmed. This will give the potatoes a warm buttery hue, and everyone likes the flavour far better than those made with milk or cream.*

Rule of thumb: When serving company, I use 1 foil stick of butter (½ cup) for roughly 3 pounds of potatoes. It's all about the flavour!

I use Yukon Gold or Mashing potatoes, as many as needed. Set into a large pot of well-salted water (1 tbsp for a large pot). When fork tender, remove, and then drain.

Cut butter into chunks and add to the potatoes. Mash with a hand masher to start, and then slowly start pouring in the evaporated milk while using an electric hand blender (up and down motion) until they're smooth and fluffy. The amount of evaporated milk used will depend on the amount of potatoes. For a large pot make sure you have 2 cans of evaporated milk on hand. You may only need a small amount from the second can, but you don't want to run short.

__Morning Potatoes__

Leftover mashed potatoes are used, and since there's usually company for breakfast at some point during the holidays, this recipe is a Godsend when it comes to convenience. I prefer this type of morning potato over all others.

Mashed potatoes, as much as desired.

Heat 2 tbsp butter and one tbsp regular olive oil **or** *3 tbsp of bacon fat in a cast iron pan. If you're cooking bacon, then you must use the fat! Anything made with bacon fat is crazy good.*

Add in desired amount of thinly sliced onion (any type you'd like), then, if you'd like, sprinkle with paprika and season with salt and pepper.

Once the onions have softened, add in the mashed potatoes and cook until potatoes have nicely browned. You may need to add in more fat to get the outer layer to nicely brown.

The Humble Christmas Salad

Ingredients

I head iceberg lettuce, chopped into nice bite-sized pieces

1 cucumber, seedless, cut lengthwise, then cut into ¼-inch pieces

2 tomatoes, large and fresh, cut in half, and then squeezed gently to remove excess juice and diced

8-10 green onions, chopped

1 cup of mayo (more can be added if needed)

Milk as needed

Salt and pepper

Directions

Chop lettuce and put into a large bowl. Add cucumber, tomatoes, and green onions. Season with salt and pepper, and then set aside until dinner is ready before adding the dressing.

In a bowl, add one cup of mayo and season well with salt and pepper. Drizzle milk in a thin stream while whisking, until the mixture is still thick but pourable — not thin and watery. Add more mayo if you've overdone it with the milk. If the dressing sits for any length of time it will thicken up, so add more milk to get it back to the right consistency.

Just before the salad goes on the table, drizzle the dressing over it while gently stirring. Use only enough to properly coat. As the salad sits on the table it will become a little soggy, which is fine, but this is a good reason not to go overboard with too much dressing initially. Taste a leaf and if it's flavourful and well-coated, it's perfect.

Claude's brother Urgel says, "Things get involved" when the mayonnaise-based salad meets up harmoniously and mingles with the meats and gravy. Sounds silly, but it's magic in the making, and no Ledoux would survive without eating this exact salad, where it belongs — directly on our Christmas dinner plates!

Christmas Cocktail Meatballs

My kids always want this appetizer when I'm hosting Christmas gatherings. I freeze them in small batches, and once defrosted, they need to be reheated slowly. A crockpot works perfect for reheating.

I make the balls fairly small in size. The last batch I made produced 110 balls. When serving, I poke them with tooth-picks to be eaten as hors d'oeuvres.

Ingredients for Meatballs

½ cup breadcrumbs

½ cup milk

1 lb ground beef

1 lb ground veal

1 lb ground pork

1 lb ground chicken

4 eggs

1 tsp freshly ground pepper

1½ tsp salt

1 tbsp garlic powder

2 tbsp oregano

½ tsp chipotle chili powder

1 tbsp olive oil per batch for frying

Ingredients for Sauce

2-680ml (about 23 oz. per each) cans of Bravo spaghetti sauce (meatless)

2–341ml (about 11½ oz. per each) jars VH Sweet & Sour Dipping Sauce

1 small tin tomato paste (5.5 oz.)

2 tbsp Italian seasoning

2 tsp garlic salt (not powder)

Directions

Mix all meatball ingredients together.

The meatballs should be "dainty," meaning one would fit nicely in a tablespoon measure.

Set heat to medium-high. Add the olive oil to a non-stick pan and fry meatballs in small batches so they aren't crowded, shaking the pan frequently. Remove from pan and set on paper towel to cool.

Mix the ingredients for the sauce and let simmer on medium-low heat for 30 minutes. Put the meatballs into a large bowl and pour the mixture over the top. Gently shake the bowl, using a silicone spatula to gently scrape sides, careful not to break them into pieces.

～

<u>Bouillée</u>

This very simple dish is basically a stew, but in summer my family refers to it as bouillée – the distinction, for me, is that it's made when locally sourced vegetables are in season – which must include freshly picked yellow and/or green beans. My recipe is more basic, but similar to the classic Pot Au Feu. Along with root vegetables (leeks and cabbage may also be used), Pot Au Feu is usually made with less tender cuts of beef (shank, for example), that require several hours of simmering, and will often include cartilaginous pieces such as marrow bones. Other versions of this dish might be made with pork hocks, and/or salted pork belly. Some will call for onions that are studded with cloves, and use nutmeg to season.

Variation for Bouillée: If I'm making it with a whole chicken instead of pieces, I'll simmer the chicken in water with cracked pepper on the stove, and then remove the meat and defat the broth. The chicken is already cooked so it's not dredged in flour. Once the broth is defatted, the meat and remaining ingredients are added.

In winter, if I'm making Beef Stew, I'll follow the Bouillée concept, but will only use root vegetables. To improve the richness of flavour, once the meat is seared, I'll add all, or at least one of the following: Half a cup of brewed black espresso coffee; a couple heaping tbsps of tomato paste; a few bay leaves (removed before serving).

Ingredients:

3 lbs chicken **or** beef chuck, cut into pieces

(GF) Flour for dredging meat (optional, but I prefer it)

Fresh cracked pepper and salt

2 tbsp olive oil and 1 tbsp butter, ghee, or margarine, more if needed to sear meat

Large bunch of fresh green and/or yellow beans, ends removed and left whole

6 or more fresh carrots, chopped

Fresh new potatoes (baby works well), unpeeled only if new, chopped into large pieces, as many as will fit into pot

1 large onion, roughly chopped

2 stalks celery, chopped (optional)

½ small turnip, chopped (optional)

1 cup cabbage, chopped (optional)

4-5 garlic cloves, minced

2 tbsp chicken or beef concentrate, depending on meat

Small bunch of fresh thyme sprigs and parsley stalks for simmering in bouillée (remove any stems before serving)

Chicken or beef broth depending on meat. Use amount needed to cover meat so it can simmer, adding more liquid to compensate for evaporation.

1-2 cups white wine (chicken), or red wine (beef), (optional)

Ingredients for Gravy Thickener

1/2 cup water
4 tbsp (GF) all-purpose flour

Directions

If simmering in oven, set at 325°F. Otherwise, simmer on stovetop on low heat.

Dredge meat in flour, if using, and season with cracked pepper and a little salt. In a large Dutch Oven, heat oil and butter (ghee, or margarine) on med-high heat, and sear meat until browned. Add vegetables, garlic, concentrate, thyme and parsley. Cover with broth and wine, if using. Bring to a boil for a few minutes, cover, and then simmer for a couple of hours. This dish is fabulous without thickening the broth, but if you'd prefer a hardier, gravy-like consistency, follow the directions below.

Directions for Gravy Thickener

Add the cold water to a glass jar with a tight-fitting lid.

Add the (GF) flour and shake thoroughly. Make certain when you remove the lid that any flour that falls from the lid is pushed down into the liquid. If you see little clumps or balls of flour, smooth out with a fork before shaking again.

Once the mixture is the right consistency you can slowly drizzle a few drops into your boiling broth while whisking constantly. Watch to see if it blends in. If you see it forming little balls of goo, your mixture is too thick, so add more water. If all is well, continue slowly drizzling in until broth reaches desired thickness.

⸈⸉

<u>My Old-Fashioned Baked Beans</u>

Beans are another of our favourite foods. Store-bought canned beans in a dark syrupy sauce are fine, but if we want this type, I just buy them as such. In this cherished recipe, they're lighter in colour, and though sweet, far less so than store-bought. Molasses added to this recipe would make a darker, richer sauce, but we prefer them without because they're more like the beans Mémère made on the farm. They freeze in small batches beautifully and make a wonderful side dish, especially at breakfast with morning potatoes.

Ingredients

Note for shopping: 1 liter or quart of chicken broth is roughly 4 cups

1 900-gram (2lb) bag of white navy beans rinsed well, and picked for pebbles or bad beans

Water

1 small cooking onion, diced

8 oz. (6-8 slices) less fatty bacon (maple flavoured optional), diced in very small pieces. (Instead of bacon, I sometimes use about 4 ounces of traditional salt pork where no additional salt brine is added. Be careful because you don't want beans to be too salty)

2 cloves garlic, minced

¼ cup ketchup

1½ tsp dried mustard

1 tbsp Demerara sugar (or brown)

6 cups chicken broth, more or less as needed to keep beans covered in liquid

Cracked pepper

About 5 splashes Frank's Red Hot Sauce, Original

2 tbsp (GF) liquid chicken concentrate

Freshly cracked pepper

Directions

Preheat oven to 325°F.

Rinse and sort beans. I do not soak overnight, but I do simmer them, which reduces cooking time in the oven. Add beans to a large Dutch Oven and then cover in water. Bring pot to boil, reduce, and allow the beans to simmer.

While simmering, use a large spoon to skim off any brown foam. Simmer until the water has evaporated to just under the top of the beans.

Remove from heat and add all ingredients, then pour in chicken broth, using just enough to completely cover the beans. Add in chicken concentrate. Taste, and add more in if desired. Season with cracked pepper.

Place the pot in the oven for 3 to 4 hours, or until the beans are cooked and the broth has thickened. Check the beans every 45 minutes or so, and if they're getting too dry add more chicken broth. If they are too soupy, tilt the lid to allow steam to escape.

<u>Simple Kick-Ass Barbeque Sauce</u>

When we're done with eating turkey, at some point during the holiday season I'll make ribs, and the sauce below is always a crowd-pleaser.

Don't worry about exact measurements with this recipe. Taste as you mix the ingredients to get the desired heat intensity. I use the sauce on pork baby back ribs. Turn the rack, bone-side up, run a knife between the bones to cut the membrane, and then remove it by pulling it away. I season my meat with chipotle chili powder, cracked pepper, garlic powder, and Cajun spice.

Ingredients

1½ cups ketchup

½ cup (GF) soy sauce

¼ cup maple syrup

Juice from a freshly squeezed lemon

Zest from ½ lemon

3 cloves of garlic, finely chopped

1 tbsp crushed chilies or cayenne pepper

1 tsp ginger

1 tsp cracked pepper

Pinch of salt

2 tbsp melted butter

Directions

Mix ingredients together. Refrigerate for several hours if possible.

Hearty Pureed Vegetable & Crispy Parsnip Soup

If I'm entertaining during the holiday season this soup is always my starter. It presents nicely with the crispy parsnip topping. Because it's hearty, it's also great to have after a day of outdoor winter activities.

Ingredients

Note for shopping: 1 liter or quart of chicken broth is roughly 4 cups

Chop vegetables trying to keep them about the same size

1 cooking onion, roughly chopped

3 carrots, roughly chopped

3 celery stalks, roughly chopped

3 potatoes, peeled and roughly chopped

½ a turnip, roughly chopped

1 large apple, or pear, roughly chopped

4 garlic cloves, peeled, smashed

Drizzle of regular olive oil

Freshly cracked pepper and a sprinkling of salt

3 tbsp (GF) chicken concentrate or other bouillon

6-8 cups of chicken broth, or more, as needed

1 cup white wine (optional)

5 sprigs fresh thyme

Dash of liquid hot sauce

Salt and cracked pepper for seasoning

Ingredients for Crispy Parsnip Topping for Soup

5-6 parsnips, or more, because they're mighty tasty, whittled into strips using a potato peeler

1 cup of canola oil

Sea Salt

Directions

Preheat oven to 425°F.

Using a large stainless-steel pan, add the vegetables, apple, and garlic cloves. Drizzle generously with olive oil and season with salt and pepper.

Set the pan in the oven uncovered, stirring frequently until vegetables are roasted and browned around the edges. If this isn't happening you can turn your oven up, but be watchful. It takes about 45 minutes in my oven. Remove the pan from the oven and let the vegetables cool.

Once the vegetables have cooled, purée in a food processor. Add in a little chicken broth if needed to blend, and then transfer to a large soup pot. Add the chicken concentrate. Cover with chicken broth, and wine if using. Add the thyme sprigs, which will be removed before serving, and season with the hot sauce. Season with salt and pepper according to taste.

Simmer the soup on the stovetop adding more chicken broth as you go along to get the consistency of broth you desire. I'll sometimes toss in a dollop of butter when simmering to add to the richness of the flavour.

Directions for Parsnip Topping

Using a potato peeler, whittle the top layer of the parsnip and discard. Continue whittling until you have a pile of thin, long parsnip pieces.

Heat oil on high in a small, high pot, until quite hot but not smoking. In small batches, using a slotted spoon, gently add the parsnip to the oil once it's hot enough that it's bubbling when the parsnip is added. Don't dare take your eyes off the pot because they'll turn crispy very quickly, going from golden brown to black in seconds. Use a slotted spoon to remove each batch to a pan lined with paper towel and sprinkle immediately with the sea salt.

When serving soup, top each bowl with a handful of the crispy parsnip and a sprinkle of thyme if you'd like.

Dessert

Denise will make dozens of sugar cookies, shortbreads and festive Christmas coffee cakes, among other goodies, lovingly garnishing each and every creation with all that sparkles. The childhood baking fiasco with the "Wedding Cake" apparently didn't traumatize her, but instead spurred her on to find joy in baking. With me, not so much!

I very rarely bake, but if I do, it's mostly butter tarts, or the odd crème Brûlée. At Christmas, a warm tart with ice cream is all you have room for after my feast anyway.

Butter Tarts

I sometimes use maple liqueur in my tarts, which is optional, because traditional butter tart recipes don't call for it. If you happen to love all things maple, and you can't find maple liqueur, simply replace a couple of tablespoons of corn syrup with pure maple syrup.

Ingredients

*½ cup raisins **or** finely chopped toasted pecans or walnuts (I prefer pecans over walnuts)*

¼ cup soft butter

¼ cup packed brown sugar

1 pinch salt

*½ cup corn syrup (traditional recipe) **or** ¼ cup corn syrup and ¼ cup (Quebec) maple liqueur **or** 2 tbsp pure maple syrup and corn syrup to make ½ cup **or** whatever makes you happy, as long as you have a ½ cup.*

1 egg, lightly beaten

½ tsp vanilla extract

Pie Dough for shells (See dough recipe)

Directions

Place raisins in a small bowl, cover with hot tap water, and let stand for 30 minutes.

In a large bowl mix the butter, brown sugar, salt, corn syrup (or any variation), until sugar is dissolved and butter is creamed.

Add egg and vanilla and mix well.

Drain and add raisins, or nuts, depending on preference.

Grease your muffin tins before setting your dough in, and then spoon mixture into the unbaked tart shells without overfilling, as the hot mixture will bubble.

Bake tarts at 400°F for about 15-20 minutes. If you prefer a firmer, less runny tart, bake for the full 20 minutes. Place on baking rack to cool.

Tarts freeze beautifully and take no more than a moment or two to defrost and warm in the microwave.

Classic Crème Brûlée

(Recipe from Holiday Edition of the LCBO magazine, 2001)

Crème Brûlée is best made in the individual gratin dishes specially designed for it, as they maximize the caramel per serving. Crème Brûlée must be made ahead and chilled, but the caramelization should be done just before serving. The broiler should be preheated so that the sugar caramelizes quickly. The best Crème Brûlée is one in which the hot sugar surface contrasts with the chilled cream. Mini-butane torches can be used instead of the broiler.

Ingredients

Makes 6

2 cups (500 ml) whipping cream

⅔ cup (150 ml) whole milk

1 vanilla bean, split lengthwise

7 egg yolks

⅓ cup (75 ml) granulated sugar

¾ cup (175 ml) light brown sugar

Directions

1. In a medium saucepan, bring cream, milk and vanilla bean to a boil. Remove from heat. Cover and leave 30 minutes to infuse.

2. Preheat oven to 200°F (100°C). Whisk the egg yolks and granulated sugar until light and thick. Whisk in cream and milk mixture, strain and then pour into 6 shallow dishes. Bake in oven about 50 minutes or until just set.

3. Let cool completely, then cover and refrigerate. (These can be made several days in advance.

4. To serve, preheat broiler, then sprinkle the surface of each Crème Brûlée with brown sugar. Broil for 2 minutes or until sugar melts and bubbles.

During the holiday season, long after the dishes have been removed, everyone remains gathered at the table listening to old stories being rehashed. Many of Papa Claude's stories relate to farm life and his wonderful dad, the late Elvida Ledoux. Pépère (as we lovingly called him), was a fiddle-playing, happy soul, known for his famous swear word "au chocolat." Although the grandkids may not yet fully appreciate the humour, or the moral of those stories, some-day, somehow, the meaning of all of them will be understood.

After a big meal, my dad always said his "sufficiency was suffunctified." As explained by linguist Frederic G. Cassidy in his article "Among the Old Words," the word, which has several variations, means "satisfied" or "satiated."

The full expression is, "My sufficiency is suffonsified and any more would be obnoxious to my fastidious taste." [v]

Part Two

Learning to Weave

V.10

ood could no longer be a unifier, a dependable distraction, a saving grace — it was an enemy, there was no war to fight to change that fact, and I was quite sure I'd forever be on the verge of tears at this particular betrayal.

The realization was finally setting in though, that there'd be no forthcoming news of a mix-up telling me that the CD test results belonged to some other crusty old hag. Now the goal, ideally, was a potential scenario where the glass could be seen as *half full* instead of *half empty*. Perspective mattered.

Before seeing the dietician to discuss the GF diet, a little hiatus was warranted. The easiest way to shut out the world was to spend it lying in bed flipping between channels. Nothing piqued my curiosity, my attention span being that of a drunken gnat — that is, until the commercials. They bloody well got my attention: the health benefits of whole grain goodness, the wonder of fibre, "I'm lovin' it burger," "finger lickin' good" chicken, "eat fresh" sub, and the neighbourhood grill with cold ale on tap – all of it toxic. I'd have preferred to be forced into painting the Sistine Chapel with a Q-tip, if once done, the reward was to return to the comfort of a life lived on my terms.

My brain must be an intricate masterpiece of complex nuttiness, so damn finely-tuned that I can rationalize how well it functions with chronic anxiety; feeling the depths of depression for the first time, however, was an entirely different matter. For those first few days I was in a dark place — in a mind closet, chain-smoking, while conjuring up images of one treasured food after another, all the foods that I'd forever see and smell, but never again taste.

Johnny Carson once said, *"I know a man who gave up smoking, drinking, sex, and rich food. He was healthy right up to the day he killed himself."* Wisely, starving as a quick way to resolve my problem was ruled out. No one chooses to live in darkness, and although there was never an apparent predisposition for depression, I still didn't want to give it space to take hold. It was time to pull myself together and make the official transition to my new life.

As I was on my way out of the dietician's office with a jam-packed information folder in hand and a large chip on my shoulder (those shoulders that carry the weight of the world on them and don't have room for a chip), she mentioned I'd become an ambassador for CD, and it took restraint not to tell her to put up her dukes so we could go a few rounds. It wasn't anything personal. She was kind, extremely knowledgeable, and certainly not flippant with me, but I was in no mood to hear this ridiculous assertion. It seemed to me it would be an eon, or two, before I'd ever entertain the idea of becoming an ambassador.

My cousin called during the mourning phase, and, when she asked how things were going, my response was that it seemed plausible that I could go into a restaurant in a wheelchair, deaf, with a seeing eye dog, my jaw wired shut and two broken arms, and have an easier time of it. Looking back, I could've taken this act to Broadway. Can anyone say Tony Award?

At the time of my diagnosis, issues related to gluten were obscure, to say the least. The management of CD through diet alone somehow made the diagnosis less believable (sadly, it still does). It sounded like some fake *designer* disease, only to be used as an attention grabber. Since there was a constant need to explain my new situation, I pulled out my imaginary wooden desk with the gum wads stuck to the underbelly, rolled up my sleeves, and found the most medically sound, reliable sources available to start my research. Inquiring minds would ask, and an addled but accurate mind would be able to answer. The dietician was right. I'd need to be my own ambassador and advocate for myself.

The fact that CD is a genetic disease particularly stuck in my craw, because all I'd ever wanted to inherit was a grand piano or maybe a condo in South Beach Miami! Nattering on is my forte, and anyone interested would learn that CD is a genetically linked autoimmune disorder with environmental triggers. (It's not an "allergy" and it's celiac disease, not "celiacs.")

If I were fraudulently parading about as a professional, I'd be telling you my official white coat is at the dry cleaners; however, in layman's terms, the information that follows is accurate, but very basic.

In someone with CD, gluten damages the hair-like structures that line the small intestine, called villi. The only way for your body to absorb nutrients is through the villi, and, without proper nutrition, you can become malnourished and susceptible to other illnesses, including certain types of cancer, which can be life-threatening. Because the disease can occur at any time, an infant, for example, born with active disease, might initially appear to have failure to thrive.

Gluten is a combo of proteins that provides wonderful elasticity and prevents crumbling in items such as baked goods. It's so damned magical that elves at the North Pole are using it on toys that require glue for assembly (the Latin word "gluten" means glue). Because of its "glue-like" properties, it can be found in a vast array of commercial applications, including non-food items.

When describing the differences within the spectrum of gluten-fueled illness there's celiac disease (CD); or the skin form, dermatitis herpetiformis (DH) that may also show damage to the villi; or non-celiac gluten sensitivity (NCGS) that does not show damage to the villi. Each group will suffer from a wide range of symptoms, and follow the same protocol as set out for CD. There are also other variables — latent, silent, and refractory, for example, which you can learn about in reliable medical publications online.

"If the stomach be irretentive of the food and if it pass through undigested and crude. And nothing ascends into the body we call such persons 'coeliacs.'"

*~Greek physician, Aretaeus of Cappadocia
(First century AD)*

DNA testing can be done which would determine if you carry the genetic marker for the disease, and you'd only need to keep a watchful eye for potential development if the marker is present. For family members of someone with CD, who are at higher risk of developing the condition, having a decisive DNA result can be valuable. Why worry if you don't have to?

Growing up, I recall Dad and some of his brothers complaining about undiagnosed digestive-related ailments. Mother was treated for a severe skin condition, thought at the time to be lupus, but I've wondered if it's possible that she had DH, commonly referred to as gluten rash, characterized by itching, stinging, and blistering. Of course, back then gluten issues weren't on a physician's radar. She'd cart Denise and me on the bus once a week to see a doctor for injections. Whatever it was, it looked like a swarm of angry bees had fed on her until they could feed no more. Her back, in particular, was a nasty mess of raised red welts.

It's six of one, half a dozen of another, trying to figure out whether my condition was inherited from Dad of Irish descent, where it's deemed to be prevalent, or from Mother, with a skin condition in an era where little was known about CD. There's no family member on either side known to have the condition, but how's it possible that there's only one defective apple in the barrel?

Initial screening for CD is blood work, and on two occasions my results were negative, which is uncommon but not unheard of. Symptoms appeared to be related to the first diagnosis of MC, but when there was no improvement with continual tweaking of the drug regimen (available to treat MC, but, as of yet, not available for CD), an endoscopy with biopsy was finally ordered.

My case presented with many of the classical signs of the disease, but it was still shocking that it took sixteen months of intolerable symptoms before a diagnosis was made. As it turns out, this was outrageously expedient, as many people wait countless years for confirmation.

CD can be hard to diagnose because some symptoms don't seem to correlate to a disease that impairs the body's ability to absorb nutrients; symptoms can vary widely, be vague, be chronic over many years, can go unnoticed, or mimic other ailments. A reliable source such as the Canadian Celiac Association (CCA) provides information on symptoms.

Let's take fatigue as an example, from the long list of possible but ambiguous symptoms. You might want to stock up on pillows when you see them on sale while waiting for an official diagnosis.

A diagnosis of "irritable bowel syndrome" can be problematic, because it's no secret that the term can be used as a catch-all phrase to describe unexplained symptoms. It's entirely possible that being labeled with this syndrome could be a contributing factor in the delay of a proper diagnosis and why the road for many tends to be quite rocky.

And, no, a chiropractor cannot see damage to intestinal villi — any more than a naturopath, podiatrist or shoe salesman can, even if you're standing before them buck-naked. And, no, you cannot diagnose CD by a skin biopsy, but you would be able to confirm the DH skin form (blood work will also be done, and it's a reasonable assumption an endoscopy could be included), or perhaps a wheat allergy, which is an entirely separate condition. And, rarely will blood screening be sufficient for diagnosis (there are some exceptions, of course, especially if there's a family history). The current gold standard method for diagnosis in adults is endoscopy with biopsy. Having said this, it's notable that research is evolving and new testing methods/protocols are on the horizon.

Self-diagnosis is tempting, especially when management of CD is strictly diet-related, and you're thinking, "Why the hell do I need a doctor to tell me that I'll feel better if I remove gluten?" Due to the stringent dietary protocol, cross-contamination issues, increased susceptibility to other conditions, and the genetic component, I'd personally think it's medically unwise to interpret how you feel as satisfactory proof of CD. Honestly, who'd want to live in self-imposed GF exile, any more than wanting to hang out in self-imposed purgatory? However, empathy is called for, for those caught between a rock and a hard place, knowing they feel better when eating GF, and afraid of the mandatory gluten ingestion required before a biopsy to avoid a false-negative result.

There are still questions related to gluten issues that may not be answered before Bigfoot is found, yet my cup would still runneth over with wisdom on the topic of living GF. It turns out it's worth taking my time to share what I've learned because misinformation is passed along quicker than a bong at a frat party.

And, surely, someone would appreciate being brushed up on gluten issues, especially during a lively discussion at a dinner party where the subject is inevitably mentioned. They could thank me later for their artful mastery of tastefully vacillating the conversation between bowel issues and Trumpian politics.

$\mathcal{V}.11$

"It's not denial. I'm just selective about the reality I accept."

~*Bill Watterson*

$\mathcal{M}$ayo clinic regarding triggers for dormant CD: "after surgery, pregnancy, childbirth, viral infection or severe emotional stress." [vi]

It seems a bit self-indulgent to write about intimate matters, but it's important to spread awareness of how someone with an unknown predisposition, like me, can get through life unscathed by life-threatening illness, and yet a culmination of events, and unexpected emotional upset, can manage to tip the applecart, causing the dormant CD beast to awaken out of hibernation.

The following passage is what transpired leading to diagnosis, and it should be a cautionary tale for anyone aware that they have a predisposition, or anyone with unexplained symptoms, since CD is considered a hidden epidemic — the majority of patients still undiagnosed.

In the course of a few short years, I'd gone through two back surgeries, five minor breast surgeries, and a complete hysterectomy. The second back surgery was a spinal fusion that came with shiny new hardware, followed by an arduous recovery.

During this period of mayhem, Claude had come through his own ordeal following a diagnosis of prostate cancer. The big "C" threw us into quite the tailspin, to put it mildly, and a hasty decision was made to go ahead with a prostatectomy. There may have been alternative therapies put on the table, but being diagnosed at such a young age meant that, regardless of how good the odds were with other less radical options, they simply weren't good enough.

Although my breast surgeries were minor in nature, each procedure brought a unique set of circumstances with healing issues (the yet-to-be diagnosed CD might explain this). Waiting for biopsy results was also stressful, always wondering when my luck would run out. And, how could there possibly be this much fuss for a "pancake" gal like me who had longingly waited for something, anything, to sprout, but, alas, was left un-endowed? On a lighter note, there's a joke that goes something like this: A woman in a lingerie department, exasperated looking for a proper fitting bra, rips open her shirt and demands that the clerk figure out what the hell she needs. The clerk, needing her reading glasses, looks closely and then asks, "Have you tried an acne product for the two blemishes?"

The hysterectomy brought on surgically-induced menopause. Changes that signal the menopausal phase, like mood swings, night sweats and hot flashes, will normally occur gradually over time, but, following surgical removal of the ovaries, the onset is usually abrupt and symptoms can be more severe. Let me tell you, the changes that arrived were an unwanted gift from Pandora.

No wonder the only remotely comical reference found for this procedure is a cartoon (author unknown), where the woman tells her husband the doctor has told her that following the hysterectomy, she won't be able to have sexual relations for six weeks, and the husband responds, "What did the dentist say?" *Bless the innocents who don't get this!*

This menopause debacle might explain why a man, confused by the onset of his better half's irrational demeanour, escapes being in her presence whenever possible. You may have come across him! He's the hatless guy driving erratically in an open-rooftop convertible during a storm on a treacherous road that should be closed. And sure, old tail-dragging Sparky might not be sparky at all, but he knows enough to jump in and ride shotgun. In Sparky's mind, if anyone's going to bark, it should be him, and he's rightfully insulted at the unpleasant usurping of his duties.

There were days I felt like that log in the bottom of the sea, with the core of my trunk hollowed out. I was no longer strong and sure of myself, hating the stark reality of knowing for certain I'd arrived at the undesired and unavoidable end of the vibrant female spectrum. If fruit were used to describe the beauty of being a woman, they wouldn't be ripe, dripping with dewiness, but dried and colourless. If flowers were used, they wouldn't be daisy-fresh. The hot flashes symbolized glowing red embers needing constant dousing, and it felt like it was only a matter of time before the flares would subside, nature returning me to dust.

With menopause in full swing, a long-distance walk at least three times a week was mandatory. It was the best prescription for keeping my raging symptoms from finally developing into something requiring the services of a criminal lawyer to untangle. Wink, wink, I'm kidding, of course!

Not only did walking lift my battered spirit, it was also instrumental in assisting with recovery from back surgery. I'd never be the lead dancer in Swan Lake, but opting for a cozy cocoon with a box of bon-bons in one hand and a remote control in the other wasn't an option.

Our medical situations created the perfect storm and changed Claude and me in unexpected and profoundly personal ways, but fortunately our relationship wasn't based on unrealistic assumptions. Nor was it based on vanity, which in all cases is a thin veneer that eventually erodes to expose a more accurate view of the human condition. It turns out it's far wiser to work on the foundation of a relationship, instead of creating short-lived optical illusions.

Finally, we got to a point where we felt confident that for the most part our medical woes were behind us. But the relief was short-lived. Although I absolutely loved my now svelte shape, I wasn't dieting, and there was no denying something was seriously wrong. I'd have to soon face reality.

My yet-to-be diagnosed symptoms appeared after the hysterectomy. My bowel decided it was now going to convert solids into its own creative concoction, which then led to fatigue, brain-fog, and drastic weight loss. At one point, hospitalization was necessary for rehydration due to potential kidney issues. It was becoming increasingly apparent my body was having serious issues mending even the smallest of nicks, cuts, blisters, bruises, and mouth cankers. And simple infections became stubborn, long drawn out affairs to clear up.

Since the only bathroom I'd want to see when everything consumed shot through me at lightning speed was located in my own private space, the house became my gilded birdcage.

On a few occasions, venturing out proved to be nothing more than foolish folly. Terror was being caught in Ikea with my bowel roaring — but, trust me, not with laughter. It was an Ikea so big you could move in with your pot-bellied pig Peppy and no one would notice. When the restroom was finally in sight, there was an out-of-order sign. The ordeal was dealt with, and luckily no one witnessed the spectacle of human combustion before it was all said and done.

It's sometimes hard to pinpoint which condition (MC or CD) causes ongoing flare-ups. It's as if my damned body's toiling away at some pointless, unending assignment. To keep things somewhat manageable for sanity's sake, at bedtime the visual of a Mariachi band is conjured up, and, being in my employ, ordered to be clad in Chip & Dale outfits. In my mind the image helps counteract the reality that I'm not in the driver's seat with an aggravated bowel that robs me of sleep. The band merrily marches along through the pipeworks toward the exit door, and finally, when their repertoire of songs has been sung, it's time to get out of bed and run to the bathroom. Sometimes, conjuring up ways to turn down the volume of their merriment suits me, but sometimes my mind drifts back to Northcliffe Boulevard in Toronto.

I'm as free as a shitty pigeon to write what pleases me, but there's no need to be insensitive, so, admittedly, there's a bit of regret wrapping up the topic of embarrassing bowel matters with an incident involving Mother. Clearly, it's unrelated to the topic at hand, apart from the fact that it involves a bathroom, but there's just no better time than now to forgive her for a debacle back in the '60s...

My parents could ill-afford the luxury of calling a serviceman, and it was a blessing that Mother had an uncanny knack for repairing things at no cost and with little fuss, but no amount of determination on her part could fix our only toilet, which was hopelessly clogged.

How cruel it is that there's still a lingering discomfort when recalling, with acuity, the day of the plumber's visit. Surely, it must have pained her to pull me aside from my playmates on what was nothing short of a stellar summer day to inform me of the shocking news. After careful assessment of the situation, the plumber, speaking in hushed confidence, to be sure, and no doubt following the strict protocol as set out in the plumbers' official manual of "Polite & Tactful Behaviour," informed her that I, Colette, was the source of the problem. Well now, the plumber had informed her of this? My, my, what a sage and insightful plumber!

It would be nice to think the problem was more directly related to the amount of toilet paper used for pampering, and certainly not because of my stockiness. Admittedly, maybe my presence at an Italian dinner table happened more frequently than it seemed.

Here's my working theory as to why the blame landed on my shoulders: With it being all about the optics with Mother, one can imagine her discomfort at having a stranger, a strapping lad of the opposite sex, in uniform, observing a clog, up close, that she couldn't pretend was a few pounds of chipped beef. It was what it was. She was quick-thinking and would need a scapegoat to assign blame. The culprit couldn't be Dad, who was grudgingly paying the bill, nor Denise, the golden child. Nor, she herself, saintly, Divine actually, never having used the mortal contraption. Therefore, the "Bull-In-The-China-Shop" and last in the pecking order would take the fall. And there was no worry I'd try to contradict her should the matter be aired publicly, considering the news had come via professional advisement. Damn, it cannot be denied that the woman was clever!

And, so it goes. There's no need for a fiddle, but there's sure a lot of fiddling about when it comes to managing the unpredictable nature of intimate matters.

Throughout our marriage, especially when there's a bit of turbulence, illnesses as described, or otherwise, it's always been a matter of mindfully practicing patience. Claude, lucky for me, is blessed with an abundance of it, which explains how he survives living with a curly-haired funnel cloud who's now focused on bowel-related problems and chin plucking (how sweet, that he still reminds me that I'm beautiful). If something bothers us, there's always a healthy bantering of viewpoints. There's a reason they haven't modified cannons for at-home use, because an occasional send-off would leave things unresolved – one of us dangling, and the other one flying over wheat fields in Nebraska. At other times, if one of us drives the other batty, it's a simple matter of immediately reflecting on our own shortcomings. Sounds corny, but good fortune is celebrated by shutting out the world so we can dance and flirt and laugh and kiss, and then dance some more. And we hug, because hugs help to fix everything. We cherish each other, as best friends do, faithfully, so mutually agreed upon commitments fall into place with ease. Struggles aren't allowed to overshadow our blessed capacity to overcome. *We both have a good sense of humour, which might be our most important joint asset.*

Joy is always found in the small graces extended, and below are a couple of examples that highlight why…

Following my second back surgery, Claude stepped into the role of nurse and chef, which meant he'd have to expand on his soup repertoire (thankfully, CD-related issues weren't yet a complicating factor). He didn't need to worry about tending to his sweet tooth because his mom and sister Diane would regularly deliver fresh fruit along with a homemade lemon meringue pie, which, if I'm going to indulge with a treat, is my hands-down favourite.

Each evening, he puttered about in the kitchen preparing dinner. Once it was ready, we'd eat at the tall café table he'd set up with one chair for him, while I'd stand. He used a small tablecloth and a candle was lit, which seemed like a considerable amount of fuss when serving someone hopped up on drugs and in pajamas.

Being on bedrest didn't allow me to witness his culinary expertise, but on my first night home he simply couldn't have produced the signature pasta dish stamped with his personal flair by opening a jar, and, believe me, the guy has an overabundance of flair. He's more than earned the nickname "Captain Claude."

His culinary skill was fabulous, but after several nights it was becoming undeniably obvious that he was using the same template as the first dinner served, because each one that followed was eerily similar. Since he continued with the Italian theme, he could do no wrong, and I was grateful that he was taking such good care of me.

We were just over a week in when he thought he'd change things up, and he proudly set an eye-appealing entrée in front of me. After a couple of bites, I realized the brown gravy formulation had been made with, yes, you guessed it, the same tomato pasta sauce he started out with on the first night.

I'll bet any trained chef would be stumped at how he managed to make the conversion.

How big a pot of signature sauce did he make on that first night, I wondered. And is there a chance it may now have botulism? And how am I going to break it to him that if he serves one more dinner with his signature sauce as the base, I'm opting out of his meal plan and will survive solely on lemon pie?

I'm pulling your leg, of course, because I would've eaten whatever was served up by this gorgeous man (with his enviable thick, wavy, mop-top head of hair, and famous white bushy mustache), as long as our lives weren't in jeopardy.

Apart from the dinners Claude made with his magical pasta/gravy invention, another dinner stands out. I was working on recipes (from Pol Martin's classic Supreme Cuisine cookbook) that were smart but simple, and aligned with my belief that a few fresh ingredients can go a long way. We'd just sat down to eat one of my new creations in the informal way we always have, but after a few bites, Claude got up from the table without saying a word, and abruptly left the room. I was less than pleased, thinking it was quite rude of him to interrupt dinner, and was ready to spew a few unmentionables at him upon his return, until he caught my eye. There he stood before me, in trousers, white shirt and tie. He'd changed from his casual top and shorts and, intently looking at me with his sparkling blue eyes, said, "A dinner like this deserves to be respected." I sat there with my apron on, stunned.

Small acts of kindness are priceless to me and will stand out as some of my favourite moments.

*"A day of joy at our daughter Kristina's wedding
to Christopher Walkling"
Walkling Farm, Muskoka region, Sept. 26, 2009*

V.12

"'Tis an ill cook that cannot lick his own fingers."

~William Shakespeare

I've come a long way, but I'm going to do a bit of reminiscing because navigating uncharted waters was part of the gastronomic journey.

With the GF lifestyle all the rage, and food manufacturers capitalizing on the trend, someone newly diagnosed should not feel too isolated or bewildered. For me, initially, I felt safer shopping at the local health food store where the items they carried were certified GF. There'd be a shelf with a couple of dusty GF cereal boxes — organic cornflakes and rice puffs. There was a smattering of other items, and it was clear they were in the fringe category, almost certain to also be egg, lactose, soy, yeast, sugar, cholesterol, fructose, MSG, colour, fat, nut, shellfish and preservative-free, and non-GMO. And it was going to cost me a small fortune for an item more suitably used for lining a cat's litter box. Imagine that, healthy, to be sure, but made from what? One would need to have a fetish for slathering peanut butter on foam sponges or cutting Styrofoam pool noodles into the length of hot dog buns, for example, to find any of it acceptable for human consumption.

A health food store is a fine place to find something herbal for constipation, but it didn't come close to replicating shopping for *real* food in a *real* grocery store. The grocery store was still useful for meat and produce, but unlike the products available now, at the time there'd be one lousy brand of bread labeled GF in vacuum-sealed plastic wrap. As it turned out, opting for the herbal constipation compound (in the health food store) was the better choice if flavour and texture mattered.

The lousy products from the health food store guaranteed that the recipes they were used in produced lousy results. I'm mentioning these fiascos because novel and obscure solutions were, by lucky accident, mastered for everyday problems. You might be delighted to find that some have the potential to come in handy, and I'm happy to pass this information along.

Right out of my kitchen, without having to trot through a forest in Portugal, cork was replicated using GF ingredients for making turkey stuffing. It wasn't edible, but certainly my ingenuity at managing this feat would have won me first prize at a science fair.

Need a quick fix for caulking? Try the first mayonnaise-based sauce I created. It could be applied like toothpaste and would dry like silicone. You'd be good to go.

If you're in a hurry to rid yourself of pesky in-laws, try the recipe used for my first batch of homemade buns. With the buns tasting overly sweet, dinner and dessert were served at the same time. Here's your hat – what's your hurry?

As mentioned earlier, apart from the butter tarts at Christmas, baking is not my thing. With plenty of stark reminders of my ineptitude, I still wanted to try my hand at making a GF Black Forest cake (even though it was odd that the recipe called for Dr. Pepper pop). Try as they might, my guests couldn't get their forks to cut through the rubbery creation, determining I'd created something NASA could use for sealing the space shuttle. With my novel invention, an astronaut could fly about worry-free with the utmost confidence.

As for baking in general, and cake in particular, my overriding sentiment persists: I will not bake one in my house, I will not bake one for Miss Mouse, I will not bake one from a box, I will not eat one with a fox. I will not bake – for fuck's sake!

Dried GF pasta made from potato flour resulted in the perfect consistency for wallpaper paste. The candlelit table was set, the simmering sauce was perfection, and in a bat of an eye, the noodles slithered down under the boiling water, never to be seen whole again. It's a damn good thing the wine was great!

When my official Canadian Celiac Association (CCA) pocket dictionary arrived, I mused over the notion that, once again, a participation award included in the package would've been a nice gesture – maybe not a piñata filled with nerve pills, but perhaps a GF chocolate brownie laced with ganja bud.

When grocery shopping before CD, I was in the habit of looking for brands I preferred, but I'd now have to examine complex lists of ingredients, most of which I couldn't pronounce. It's a marvel that grocery stores don't implode into damning infernos, because many ingredients, no doubt, could be used in formulations for products like lawn fertilizer.

I'd courageously leave for the grocery store armed with my dictionary, and a hanky for unexpected moments when tears would sprout (this usually occurred when inhaling freshly baked bread from the open bins). I was like Sherlock Holmes hot on a case searching for clues in the soup aisle, stealthily moving the mission forward. All that was needed to complete the look was a derby hat, a pipe, and that groovy blue vinyl cape Mother had made me back in the '60s. Canadian labelling laws now require that gluten in any ingredient in the formulation must be stated, resolving this issue, but I'm now focused on ferreting out sugar/sucrose, high-fructose corn syrup, dextrose, and other countless ways it's listed, and hidden. Once I've mastered the sugar angle, I look forward to the day when I'm only searching for pine-cones in pine trees.

Once my cupboards were jam-packed with the vast array of ridiculous GF replacement items — an assortment of flours ground from God-knows-what, egg replacer, xanthan or guar gum, and other foreign materials needed to replicate normal gluten laden foods — the only other requirement was to stay organized. The following musings relate to kitchen matters, some of which are sensible regardless of whether gluten is an issue:

Uncluttered kitchen counters have always been impor-tant to me. Older sister Lynn would pop by the house on Northcliffe Boulevard for impromptu sit-ins, hopping up to plop her ass on the counter in a spot that should've been reserved for the ingredients needed for sauce, as it would be at Signora's. Though she had no way of knowing this, and maybe unjustifiably, the contradiction between Signora's counter content and ours irked me a bit.

The goal now, in my GF kitchen, is to avoid the possibility

of contamination from outside sources — pristine is the aim. This means everyone should avoid bringing in foods containing gluten, nor shall they park their ass, keys, bills, techie things, reading glasses, purses, et cetera on my limited counter space. I'll admit, though, having bills in plain sight might be a decent diet strategy because the only thing they're good for is taking away your appetite.

It would be wise to avoid ordering goofy gadgets from television advertisements, the shopping channel, or infomercials. Few items are designed with the specific aim of making GF cooking goof-proof. If the temptation is getting out of control, I say, "Colette, step away from the phone (or computer)." All previously must-have gadgets didn't make the cut, and the novelty wears off before the credit card statement arrives. A lovely signora living in my old neighbourhood would've had time to prepare two bushels of tomatoes, weed the garden, and make lasagna for a funeral buffet in the same time it takes me to open, assemble parts, read instructions, and toss the item into the cupboard. I always promise myself to use a gadget a couple of days after purchase, but rarely has this happened.

Try to never be fooled into buying a boxed set of anything. Who needs forty pots and pans that will have dangling handles in less than six months, fancy glass lids, steamer basket, strainer, an array of plastic utensils, and a complimentary cookbook, all tantalizingly marketed with a sexy chef's endorsement, and all for a ridiculously low price? Unless said chef will step out of the gigantic box when opened — resist.

No one wants to blow the budget, understandably, but it's cheaper in the long run to buy better quality appliances. Don't be convinced otherwise by a spiffily dressed salesman with a smile so bright he's a shoo-in for Rudolph. Personally, I cannot be inspired to cook and create using appliances that aren't much better than glorified Fisher Price toys. There was no Easy Bake Oven found under the Christmas tree as a kid, and I sure as hell don't want one now.

If I remodel my kitchen it'll include another warming drawer because they're the greatest invention since the toaster. And should the electrician request the Picasso I may inherit as payment to install it — the painting will be gladly handed over. Such is life.

Never forget that bed skirts (decorative fabric sheets draped over the box-spring to hide it) are versatile if you happen to be caught without a decent tablecloth. My only caveat: do not attempt this if guests are royalty or Martha Stewart. If an aromatic meal is served on charming platters, no one will notice what's covering the table. To be on the safe side, it also doesn't hurt to be serving good wine, and dining by candlelight. Been there, done it!

Decent cutlery is a must! Spoons shouldn't bend from the heat of a bowl of soup, and fork prongs shouldn't look like they've been used to adjust the innards of an antique appliance. I'll never forget the Christmas Mother gave me a gift of cutlery. A few months later she'd come for a short visit, and, while she was setting the table for dinner, she started to rant and rave. "My God, Colette, who in hell would buy this worthless damn cheap cutlery?" I was more than pleased to fill her in on the details.

Water and wine glasses should glitter. Dishes can be retro-chic, but, if they're chipped and scratched and appear to have been used to feed the dearly beloved, melodramatic, bit of a snoot, Cardigan Welsh corgi, restocking is in order. (RIP Miss Sadie)

One more quirky suggestion nicely highlights living with fretfulness. When you're cooking for company, the food needs to be presented in the best way possible, so save the disposable plastic shower caps found in hotel rooms for donning while food prepping. The alternative to this method is the notion of needing to use the Heimlich maneuver because a dinner guest is choking on a hair that's tangled around a perfectly grilled piece of beef, and then watching the dislodged meat that's now a projectile knock a candle over, thus requiring a fire extinguisher. Always thinking, and always a method to my madness!

To be sure, anything that's in my direct control is the easiest to manage. It may have taken years, perhaps it was stubbornness, but eventually things settled into place and cooking at home was once again a joyful experience. And, when company is gathered, my communal table is as fine a sight as any I've seen.

Dishes that were adaptable to a GF conversion were getting better over time. How bad could things be? A raccoon with a highly developed palette from a broad exposure to a cornucopia of culinary delights followed the scent wafting from my kitchen, and, to my surprise, was comfortably lounging on the seasonal loveseat on the upper back deck. He needed to crawl along the hedge and over the railing because there aren't any stairs, which meant he was determined to get here. Unfortunately, he didn't make a prior dinner reservation. You'd think he'd have already figured out, that, without one, he's not welcome, but I'll take his visit as a compliment!

V.13

My first short jaunt following diagnosis will endure as a lasting reminder that trying to navigate in a gluten-laden world with shyness, tears, and my tongue in my back pocket would only get me to the square root of zero. Interestingly, a group of us were on our way to a seminar based on *The Secret*, the wildly popular book about using the Law of Attraction to achieve the life you desire.

I'd started out feeling quite beautiful that day. My perfectly pleated crisp black skirt had a wide swatch of beige bordering the hem, which matched my black shoes with beige button and piping. My purse was also black, with beige retro flower appliqués that would've gone nicely with those beloved go-go boots I had back in the '60s. All was well, but Claude had given me a little insulated blue bag with a logo (it had come as a freebie with a case of beer) for my GF sandwich, and it did worry me that this necessary but unfashionable accessory might make me look ridiculous. In the end I entered the seminar, meticulous outfit intact, culinary safety net in the car.

Our lunch break was less than an hour, not enough time to seek out GF options, and it only made sense for me to separate from the others. As they went off in search of lunch, I headed out to find a valet who was tipped handsomely for retrieving the car mid-event, and I returned to the hotel with my small blue eyesore.

The main floor was under renovation and seating was scarce, but there was a cordoned-off area where guests could get food service, and the remaining chair beckoned. Two haughty ladies seated next to me were giving me the dreaded Evil Eye, no doubt appalled at the sight of my tacky cooler bag.

Within moments, a waiter was asking me to leave the area as it was reserved for paying customers only. He didn't even bother to first inquire if I'd like a drink of some sort. (Come to think of it, maybe he thought my cooler was stocked with beer!)

It wasn't a good scenario for someone who's painfully shy, and I did my utmost best to look unfazed while walking away. And no, I wasn't at all looking like a model strutting on a New York City runway during Fashion Week, but more like a gimping fraud caught in a spotlight with spinach in her teeth and a snag in the arse of her frock.

Ravenous — my last meal had been an omelet served without bread the night before — and running out of time, I sought refuge at a sofa table located outside the elevator banks. And there before me was the truth: my recently minted status as a celiac signalled the end of dining out with mindless ease. The GF bread had crumbled and now resembled clumps of peat moss. The confused valet once again retrieved the car, the cooler bag was ditched, and then it was back to the seminar, feeling hungry and defeated.

In the years since, I've put in oodles of miles test-driving the GF lifestyle. At times, I've been fortunate to receive personal attention from renowned chefs in some of the finest dining establishments. But, as a matter of survival, I've found myself scouring for something safe to eat from dilapidated gas stations, where I'm pretty sure I saw buzzards circling overhead. I've received rock star treatment, felt like a hapless beggar, and experienced every conceivable dining scenario sandwiched in between.

Claude tries to circumvent dining debacles whenever possible. If we're visiting a new city and have made a reservation, he'll try to stop by the restaurant earlier in the day. A frazzled chef without time to prepare doesn't make for a merry evening. In his wonderful, endearing French accent, he'll tell the maître d' his wife is a "Glooten." It's touching beyond words and more than admirable, but I'll laugh, reminding him that I might be a bit odd, but there's no such thing as a "Glooten." He claims through experience that when it comes to affairs such as dinner reservations, he's tired of saying his wife is a celiac, as the maître d' stares bewildered, likely thinking I should be somewhere under locked supervision.

No restaurant should have to accommodate my dietary needs. Period. But, when they manage to, with care, it's humbling. Thankfully, progress has been made, but guidelines are still needed for the smoothest sailing possible, especially when no advance notice to the restaurant has been given.

Cross-contamination issues are dealt with before being seated, to avoid making a scene. Claude loves me, but being in the company of a hungry, pissed-off funnel cloud in front of nosy tourists, their fingers poised over the video button on their iPhones, is not what he signed up for.

The now commonplace "Gluten Friendly" menu is not a safe bet, but thankfully I've managed to unpack the regular one while avoiding the expectation of a miracle. For example:

"Herb Crusted Chicken Breast with Cranberry and Wild Rice Stuffing, Spicy Rum Compote, Garlic Baguette and Garden Salad drizzled with In-House Dressing."

What I get: a piece of chicken and garden salad, minus everything else, including the in-house dressing.

The reality is that it's safer to avoid eating in food venues at peak dining hours, especially during their busy season. If we've made no prior arrangements, it's almost impossible to order a safe dinner by bellowing my needs to a waitress, when the band's blaring amplifiers are cracking the rattling dentures of dinner guests.

My goal from the start was to reach a state of acceptance so I could then transition to a more emotionally stable state – that of adaptation. Things are sometimes easier said than done.

V.14

Obedience when following my new lifestyle regimen was exemplary, but it was expected that at some point there'd be a glitch. The winter had dragged on for eternity, and the yellow ball referred to as the sun was nothing more than a tease, popping out only long enough to look heavenwards while praying for spring. I loved Claude for suggesting we spend a few days at an inn for a change of scenery, but something told me this little jaunt might be tricky to navigate. Considering this was my first trip going a little further afar, and in the company of a man who insisted on eating GF to make my life easier and might now be severely craving gluten-laden delights, any temptation might set me off course. On occasion over the years, I've prepared dinners such as prime rib of beef, beef bourguignon, coq au vin, and rack of lamb, to name a few, which befitted any restaurant table, but it's always magical to have someone else wear the apron while I dedicate the rare experience to memory.

We were warmly welcomed upon arrival to a hearth with crackling fire in an ancient, high-ceilinged room of stone and timber and accented with the ancestral owner's portrait hanging prominently. I avoid staring at old portraits, fearful of evoking the wrath of a spirit who might find my nosy inspection disrespectful. I also don't care how swanky or posh a place is; my preference is to sleep with one eye open on the watch for anything that has more than two legs. Adding an angry spirit to my watch would require both eyes open and defeat the purpose of a rejuvenating retreat.

Sure enough, as with any inn worth its salt, the best feature was the dining room. It had an unpretentious, casual feel, but the attention to detail didn't go unnoticed: luxurious table linens; weighted silver cutlery that one could pretend came from the founding lady's heirloom collection; glistening oversized stemware; a view of the courtyard where the lanterns' soft glow seemed to be warming the snow-covered flagstone; and a snappy little candle on the table, its flame dancing in sync with the softly-played jazz standards.

With a Manhattan working its way through my veins, pretending to be no different than anyone else in the room was getting easier by the minute. No call was made in advance of our visit, or mention made to the waiter when seated that they'd be dealing with a "Glooten," and it didn't take long before the words spilled out: "I can't help myself, I'm going to do it, and I hate myself for the lack of willpower."

The building shook when the bread arrived. As expected, the assortment of artisanal bread had been properly tucked into a white linen cloth to keep it warm. Thank God a cocky chef didn't opt for a healthier, more modern version of the standard bread offer. Claude could've channelled Mr. Bean and picked his nose with his salad fork after removing earwax with a swizzle stick, and I wouldn't have noticed. Each chunk of broken bread was chewed slowly, with eyes closed.

It was naively hopeful to think the dinner would cause no harm. The gluten-laden bread, sauces, and dessert were attempting to commandeer their way through their hostile new environment, and the guilt arrived with the dinner tab.

It's hard to truly savour something that's forbidden, on top of worrying about what'll happen if the built-up will-power needed to resist further temptation is lost. With countless failed attempts at smoking cessation under my belt I was all too aware of the possibility of falling off the compliance wagon.

The vision of feeding a gluten addiction by hiding in a closet with a loaf of bread, in the dark and with no ventilation, should serve as a sufficient deterrent. One can always hope, right?

It was cheating — pining for a romantic, normal dinner, and managing to break every rule in the GF bible. What would it take to repent from my glutinous, sinful escapade? Not sure, but the only seemingly sensible option at the time was to silently chant the Hail Mary and Our Father and then call on angels with as much reverence as could be mustered in my poisoned state. This indiscretion couldn't be the start of another bad habit.

Dr. Ivor Hill, Section Chief of Gastroenterology and Director of the Celiac Disease Center at Nationwide Children's Hospital, had this to say about cheating: "Continued or repeated cheating on the diet will lead to progressive damage, and we know that in some cases, this can be fairly extensive for some years before clinical signs develop."

Another aspect of an overactive imagination is the habit of silently praying. For me, this is more about spiritual mindfulness than any certainty that my petition is being heard. I sense the angels are close by, but I haven't a clue whether God is upstairs listening intently or ignoring us because He's peeved at how we've completely screwed things up (I'm thinking specifically here about our mistreatment of the environment). But in case He turns up at an Ikea to replace the worn-out furniture He thunderously drags around when it's stormy, I'm giving Him a shout-out. And, as for Mary, I just love her! A woman who gave birth in a frosty manger and then entertained three wise men who probably expected dinner is a hero in my eyes!

George's Prime Rib of Beef

Ask the butcher to "French" the meat (cut away fat and meat from the bone) for you, and allow for about one pound per person. A thermometer is essential.

Ingredients for Marinade

4 tbsp butter

⅓ cup Italian parsley, chopped fine

1 tbsp chives, chopped fine

1 tsp mint, chopped fine

2 tsp basil, chopped fine

2 tsp rosemary, chopped fine

2 cloves garlic, minced fine

8 tbsp gin (4 oz.)

¾ tsp allspice

Ingredients for Wine Sauce

2½ cups Pinot Noir, or substitute with Cabernet Sauvignon or Syrah

4 cups (GF) beef stock. You can use beef broth but stock is more suitable for flavour.

Directions

Melt butter in saucepan and add herbs, garlic, gin and allspice. Sauté until well stirred. Set aside one tablespoon of marinade for later use.

Trim roast of excess fat (if butcher did not prepare the meat), then cover with herb marinade. Cover and refrigerate for at least an hour, but preferably as long as twelve hours. Remove from fridge and bring to room temperature — an absolute must.

Preheat oven to 425°F. Place roast fat side up in pan and cook for 20 minutes. Reduce oven temperature to 350°F and cook until internal temperature reads 125°F (130°F internal temperature would be rare, but I prefer to remove the roast a little sooner to ensure it doesn't over-cook). Remove roast from oven and loosely tent with foil for 20-30 minutes. Do not carve until it has fully rested for maximum tenderness.

While meat is resting, add wine to saucepan and gently boil until it's reduced to a ¼ cup. Add beef stock. When it has reduced to the point that the liquid has thickened and is clinging to the spoon, add the one tablespoon of left-over marinade.

Alternative method: I'll bring a prime rib to room temperature, and then slather it in a mixture of butter, cracked pepper, Dijon mustard, garlic, and Herbs de Provence. I'll multiply the weight of the roast by 5. (For example, a 6-lb roast would be 30 minutes). I preheat the oven to 500 F° and cook the roast for the amount of time calculated. The roast is probed, and the oven is turned down to 175° F and the oven door is not opened for the duration of the cooking time. When my probe reaches 120-125° F the roast is removed and it's rare. Once it rests, it's a perfect medium rare to serve. In the summer we'll also use the Green Egg, or barbeque the roast on the spit.

Beef Bourguignon

I've had this recipe for years and would love to give credit where credit is due, but I can't recall who passed it along to me. I don't know if this recipe is close to the classic French dish, but it will more than impress your guests. Put on your apron, pour yourself a glass of wine, play some old-fashioned French classics and enjoy. Bon appétite.

Ingredients

8 ounces bacon, coarsely chopped

3 lbs well-trimmed boneless beef chuck cut into 1½-inch cubes.

⅓ cup (GF) all-purpose flour

1¼ lbs pearl onions

¾ lb large carrots cut into 1-inch pieces

12 large garlic cloves, peeled but left whole

3 cups beef broth

½ cup cognac or brandy

2 bottles red Burgundy wine, or substitute with a Bordeaux or Beaujolais

1¼ lbs white mushrooms, whole or sliced in half

⅓ cup fresh thyme, chopped, or 2 tbsp dried

1 tbsp dark brown sugar

1 tbsp tomato paste

Directions

Preheat oven to 325°F

Sauté bacon in heavy large Dutch Oven until it's brown and crisp — about 8 minutes.

Using slotted spoon, transfer bacon to paper towel.

Season beef generously with salt and pepper. Coat beef with flour.

Working in small batches, brown the beef in the bacon fat over high heat until seared, about 5 minutes per batch.

Transfer meat to large bowl with the bacon.

Add onions and carrots to the pot and sauté until light brown, about 6 minutes.

Add garlic to vegetables and sauté about 1 minute.

Transfer vegetables to the bowl with the beef.

Add one cup broth and cognac to the pot and gently boil it until it's reduced to a glaze while scraping up the browned bits, about 6-8 minutes.

Return meat, vegetables, and their juices to the pot.

Add wine, mushrooms, thyme, sugar, tomato paste and the remaining two cups of broth. Bring to a boil, stirring occasionally.

Cover pot and place in oven at 275°F for approximately 2 hours, or until meat is fork tender.

Remove from oven and ladle off the fat on top and discard, then ladle the liquid from the stew into a large saucepan, leaving the meat and vegetables to sit, covered. Gently boil liquid until reduced to about 2¾ cups, about 30-40 minutes.

Season with sea salt and freshly cracked pepper.

Pour liquid back over the meat and vegetables. Mashed potatoes are wonderful with this dish.

Coq Au Vin

The more traditional way to make this dish is using a whole chicken, skin included, cut into 8 sections. I'm certain that chef Paul Bocuse would never have entertained removing the skin because the skin would provide flavour, and fat would be considered as good as the meat itself. More modern versions of this recipe, as a matter of convenience, use a combination of skin-on chicken legs and thighs. As for our sensibilities, Claude and I prefer to create great flavour without having blubbery chicken skin cooked into the sauce. By all means, make it as it's traditionally prepared, easily done by following one of the countless recipes available online.

Ingredients

1 tbsp olive oil

*4 lbs whole chicken cut into 8 sections **or** an assortment of thighs and drums combined. I prefer to use skinless chicken.*

Beurre Manie: 3 tbsp (GF) all-purpose flour + 3 tbsp softened butter, mashed with spoon to make a smooth paste

8 oz. bacon diced fine

1 cooking onion, diced

8 pearl onions, halved (Trim the root ends and set them into a bowl of boiled water for about 10 minutes, and then rinse under cold water. Peels will be easier to remove.)

½ lb assorted mushrooms, sliced

2 garlic cloves

2 tbsp tomato paste

1 bottle dry red wine (Burgundy or something similar)

¼ cup cognac

3 cups chicken broth

6 sprigs fresh thyme

4 sprigs fresh rosemary

3 carrots, cut in large pieces — optional

Freshly cracked pepper

Directions

Marinate chicken in 2 cups of wine for several hours. Your chicken will turn pinkish red, and this is just fine. Set in fridge to marinate. Remove and bring to room temperature when ready to use.

Preheat oven to 325°F.

Make Beurre Manie and set aside.

Dice cooking onion. After soaking pearl onions, slice in half. Quarter mushrooms, and mince garlic. Set aside.

In a large Dutch Oven add olive oil, and over medium-high heat cook bacon until crisp. Remove and set aside. Remove all but 1tbsp oil from pot.

Remove chicken from wine marinade and reserve the marinade. Brown chicken seasoned with cracked pepper in small batches so they sear to a nice brown, and then remove and set aside.

Add onions, pearl onions, mushrooms and garlic. Sauté for few moments. Stir in tomato paste. Add cognac, reserved wine marinade, and the remainder of the bottle of wine. Bring heat up to get a gentle boil and stir while lifting crispy bits from bottom of pot. Stir in bacon.

Reduce heat and add chicken to pot. Add chicken broth. Add fresh thyme and rosemary.

If you are adding carrots, add them now. Not all recipes call for carrots but I prefer to add them in because they enhance the dish.

Stir in the Beurre Manie. Season with more cracked pepper.

Bake in a preheated oven at 325°F for about 3 hours.

<u>Barbequed Rack of Lamb</u>

This recipe is for two racks, with each rack having four to six bones. For best results, start marinating in early morning for meat that will be barbequed in the evening. This recipe was passed along by my brother-in-law George decades ago, and I have no idea of where he originally obtained it.

Ingredients for Marinade for Meat

4 tbsp butter

1 tbsp 4 peppercorn spice, ground

4 tbsp fresh thyme, minced finely

4 tbsp fresh Italian parsley, minced finely

4 tbsp fresh chervil, minced finely

4 tbsp fresh rosemary, minced finely

Ingredients for Sauce

1 cup chicken broth

1 cup beef broth

1 bottle of Bordeaux wine (Burgundy or Beaujolais can be substituted)

2 tbsp meat marinade (that you've reserved)

½ pint whipping cream

Directions

Trim off any excess fat from racks.

In a saucepan, add butter with marinade ingredients, sauté for 1-2 minutes, and then remove from heat. Set aside 2 tbsp of marinade.

Apply remaining marinade to meat side of racks, and then wrap until ready to barbeque.

In a fairly large pot over medium-high heat, use the fat trimmings to glaze the pot, and then remove. Skip this step if there's no fat trimming available.

Add chicken and beef stock and bring to a boil. Let this reduce to approximately ½ to ¾ cups of liquid.

Add wine and once again bring the liquid to a boil. Turn heat down to get a gentle boil, and let the liquid reduce to approximately ¾ cup. Remove from heat.

Barbeque the lamb racks on an open flame to sear, about five minutes per side. If using a meat thermometer, when they reach an internal temperature of 140 to 150°F remove from heat, tent with foil, and allow to rest for about 15 minutes.

While the meat is cooking or ready to rest, return the liquid to the stove, add the cream and the 2 reserved tbsp of marinade and whisk. Return pot to a gentle simmer. Season with the cracked pepper and a pinch of salt.

When plating, spoon the sauce onto the bottom of each plate and set rack on top.

V.15

Receiving or giving unsolicited advice doesn't much appeal to me. But I had a moment when transcendent clarity manifested, so, if you'll indulge me, I'd like to dispense a little advice as it relates to the avoidance of health matters.

Suffering with the heavy burden of fear, I would blindly ignore an issue when it initially cropped up. This would be followed by a rationalization that it mustn't be that bad, a valiant effort to pray it away, a request for angels to intercede on my behalf, and an attempt to fix the issue myself.

Of course, there'd only be myself to blame if something serious had developed unchecked, and the irreversible "Condemned" sign was posted. Believe it or not, a bird-brained ostrich knew better than me when it came to burying his head in sand – he never did it as an act of avoidance, and never will.

Around the time of the Type II diabetes diagnosis, I was feeling pretty lousy overall, even though my blood sugar level was barely over the threshold required to make it official. I felt like I'd swallowed the frog that sat on the bump on the log in the bottom of the sea. Therefore, it stood to reason, since I was already a dandy collector of autoimmune diseases, some other godforsaken condition must be brewing.

Trying to survive, frozen in fear, while simultaneously trying to perform mental gymnastics, had become unbearable. It was time to get to work, at a feverish pace, perfecting a strategic plan that might eradicate a potential problem and might possibly reverse the diabetes, because I'd read stories that claimed it was possible. Would a far-flung regimen cure me? No damn clue.

I may have the slightest tendency to be a tad bit dramatic, so it shouldn't be surprising that I made a hasty decision to follow a ridiculously stringent cleanse/fast that looked hopeful for healing the body. There was a bit of a problem, however, because the method wasn't written in this century, and the long-deceased designer of the plan lived in Europe, where there's a much larger abundance of natural sources to work with. It called for beet juice (available), but some of the teas and herbs were foreign-sounding, almost impossible to find, and, quite possibly, extinct. It wouldn't have shocked me if the cleanse had called for a pinch of unicorn dandruff.

Wracked with worry, I decided to give it a whirl before finding a source for some of the required ingredients. Without the ability to follow the exacting standards, we still thought we were in pretty good shape to start. Claude, who's my greatest supporter, wanted to follow the process with me, even though I hadn't mentioned a word about my underlying health concerns. He's easy-going in nature, and doesn't bother questioning my eccentric ways.

Cases of beet juice manufactured in Europe were shipped from Montreal. We visited a shop in Ottawa where some of the teas and herbs were found – along with teacups painted with our Chinese zodiac symbols (a pig on mine and a horse on Claude's) needed, I'd think anyone would agree, for good luck. Other organic herbs were ordered from a large supplier in Goodwood, Ontario. Tons of organic onions were purchased, as one cup of onion broth, minus the onions, was the main food source for each day. I planted sage and purchased seeds to plant the next season. Claude thought distilled water would be essential for overall purity, purchasing enough water to keep us hydrated for the duration, with enough left over for any unforeseen Trumpian-induced disaster. We bought an electric kettle, and a thermometer, needing to ensure the tea would be consumed at a precise temperature. Blood sugar testing supplies and a blood pressure cuff were on hand.

On the first morning, I headed to the garden (actually, it's a small flowerbed in the front yard) to pluck the sage leaves. I didn't need a sickle for chopping like Nonna would use in the Old Country, but it felt like an earthy, groovy thing to do, and, in the moment, I thought perhaps my chakras (don't ask me what they are, no clue, but sounded about right) were getting tuned up. The sage needed to be steeped and gargled, and then more was needed to prepare the boiled tea brew, which was missing some of the yet-to-be sourced herbs. The beet juice was to be taken in small mouthfuls, allowing it to mix with saliva before swallowing. The onion soup was prepared and strained, and we had our lunch. At precisely set intervals throughout the day, certain teas and/or herbs needed to be sipped. We didn't feel hungry (although admittedly, I was ready for bed by noon) and therefore exclaimed that Day One of the mandatory Forty-Two-Day duration was a smashing success.

They claim that a cleanse brings mental clarity, and indeed I could only marvel at how thick my brain fog must have been before the start and how clear my mind felt the next morning. With it now uncluttered, it was only prudent to recheck the details of the regimen.

Clearly, some of the vital info had been skimmed over. And, surely, the missing ingredients would alter the efficacy of the result, wouldn't you think? I desperately wanted to cure myself, but it stood to reason, replacing one ailment with a potential scurvy-like illness was risky business.

At four o'clock we officially declared an end to our grueling escapade as a triumphant trial run. While I was still in my pajamas surveying my juice, herb, tea, and onion-filled kitchen, I was mentally seeing the picture of an illegal grow-op.

All of the perishables in the fridge had been given away a few days before (what Virgo nut-job isn't so organized?), so I'd need to shop. At the best of times, perishables are a problem – fruit, in particular. It doesn't just sit and make nice in the fridge, like a jar of mayo. Most fruit marches into my kitchen already imperfect, flips me the finger, and curses me with its Evil Eye before smugly getting comfy in the crisper. It took a bit of effort to get reorganized, but we soon settled back to a familiar routine.

As it turned out my troubling symptoms eventually dissipated. Perhaps my Chinese teacup brought me luck, but let's face it, at some point, luck can run out. As age-related illness becomes more of a reality, and conditions can tend to be more serious, it'd be prudent to be more like my Zodiac pig and less like a mule (or, more aptly stated, a jackass). A lesson was learned.

becomes more of a reality, and conditions can tend to be more serious, it'd be prudent to be more like my Zodiac pig and less like a mule (or, more aptly stated, a jackass). A lesson was learned.

It was time to zone in on sensible lifestyle changes that would help reduce the odds, if possible, of receiving yet another unforeseen diagnosis. Some of the issues that got sorted out might not stand up to medical scrutiny, but, if a regimen fits into my safe zone, there can only be an upside. If you're worried about potentially being blown away like dried tumbleweed in a windstorm because you're unwell, I wish you luck, but please do your own homework! I'm totally incapable of dispensing medical advice, nor prompting anyone to follow in my footsteps. Any symptom someone consults me for will garner the same response: "In your condition, your new tail should appear first, your hooves will come next, and use calamine lotion if itchiness develops."

Before embarking on fasting, the pros and cons needed to be considered, with information garnered from reputable sources. The health benefits are numerous but there were caveats to consider. My first "sensible" fast lasted 48 hours and was achieved using a no-nonsense approach. I simply drank lots of water, and sipped on Chaga mushroom tea (a fungus grown mainly in cold climates on birch trees) to stay well-hydrated. A headache developed by mid-afternoon on the first day which might be attributed to caffeine withdrawal. Once the headache cleared, I felt fine. My blood sugar level lowered to the normal range. Fasting or not, I drink at least 48 oz. of water a day ensuring I'm well hydrated, especially before bed, because I've read, from a cardio-vascular standpoint, it's a good idea.

In addition to the type of fast outlined above, I'm now following the "8/16" fasting routine as diligently as possible. Healthy foods are eaten within an eight-hour period during the day, and then it's fasting for sixteen hours (longer, if possible) in between.

As I mentioned earlier, even though I haven't got a sweet tooth and have rarely consumed raw sugar, it's still been a complete pain in the ass figuring out how to once again alter my diet to include the management of diabetes. The amount of sugar found in condiments, salad dressings, marinades, et cetera, shocked the hell out of me. Ditto for outrageous sodium levels, especially in Asian-type cooking sauces.

Sensibly, I devised a list of foods deemed safe, and they all must be as low as possible on the glycemic index (see GI information in Glossary).

Legumes and beans; fruits and vegetables (those with low sugar content); seeds, nuts, and grains (excluding those related to CD as follows: wheat, barley, rye, triticale, bulgar, couscous, durum, einkorn, emmer, farro, kamut, semolina, and malt derived from off-limit grains. Oats are also exclud-ed unless they're certified GF due to cross-contamination); salad greens; seafood (nothing raw, no eyeballs, no tentacles); animal meat as it's naturally GF, although I've read a recent study that suggests a vegan diet might actually be the key to controlling Type II diabetes; dairy (limited, and only if low in sugar — not recommended but I'm addicted); and wild rice (or other types with low levels of arsenic). Many GF products use rice as an alternative to wheat, so arsenic levels matter, especially for children with CD.

The Mediterranean diet is believed to be one of the healthiest ways to eat, and my diet has been roughly adjusted accordingly, although yogurt is avoided. The list below is taken from Oldways: Health Through Heritage, a non-profit food and nutrition organization.[vii]

1. Meats and sweets. To be eaten less often.

2. Poultry, eggs, cheese and yogurt. Moderate portions — daily to weekly.

3. Fresh fish and seafood. At least two times per week.

4. Fruits, vegetables, grains (mostly whole), olive oil, beans, nuts, legumes, seeds, herbs and spices. Base every meal on these foods.

One thing's for sure: it takes a lot of effort to pass the test of living with a condition that requires meticulous attention to detail. The only thing I can think of swallowing without forethought is a fly, unless, of course, it was recently sun-tanning on a gluten-laden sandwich platter at a picnic.

In my pre-diagnosis days, my idea of a resolution was *"an excuse for one last binge, followed the next day by a sincere attempt at piety with focused contemplation on sins, followed by an early turn-in for much needed restful sleep, and then back to the same old habit sometime around noon the next day."* Clearly, I needed to redefine the concept.

I've admitted to my gluten-laden cheating fiasco when having dinner at that inn shortly following diagnosis, but that was it. From a medical aspect, there's zero allowance for gluten ingestion under any circumstance. There's no TGIG – "Thank God It's Gluten-Day." There are no binges, no bites, no swiping, no excuses. Period. Should a family member develop the condition, they'll be able to look at my behaviour and see that I've set the right example. CD is no different than any other disease – following the stringent protocols is the only hope for survival.

⌒⌒

Speaking of survival, I'd watch *My 600-Lb. Life* or *Hoarders* and see life-threatening issues that were glaringly visible, where someone was one Twinkie or prized piece of toxic junk short of disaster. The shows were relatable, because someone like me, with invisible perils, potentially faces a similar fate. But there was one thing for sure: "It is what it is" would need to become "It was what it was."

Many people who have never smoked don't realize that it's not always a simple matter of dealing with a few weeks of miserable withdrawal symptoms. It's a reasonable assumption to make; then again, many assumptions appear the same right up until the moment they're proven otherwise.

When it came to dealing with my smoking habit, I'd quit for several months, or longer, and the entire time it felt like I was holding my breath, anxiously waiting for the exercise to be magically over so I could be transported back to my comfort zone. Holding my breath while breathing with smoke-free lungs is a whacky oxymoron, am I right? I already know the answer to my rhetorical question!

I don't know if there's a "best" way to overcome an unhealthy habit that brings comfort, so I won't attempt to dispense wisdom-laced truisms, many that are also nonsensical. Some will go the cold turkey route; others, the slow rollout with baby steps. Some will hold on until the dead-end of rock bottom leaves no alternative. Some, like me, would simply avoid reality. Years ago (before my CD diagnosis) a doctor told me I was quite the full-figured woman, and I was shocked. Of course, I was shocked, because the news didn't reflect the alternative reality I'd conveniently created. Gosh, my favourite things to shop for were shoes, because the mirror on the floor at the shoe store didn't expose anything other than my slim ankles and size seven feet. I never actually "looked" at my figure, except when a cursory glimpse was necessary to ensure that my standard black outfit was suitable for the occasion. The truth, I'd come to realize, is that denial comes with a pricey sales tag. What cost was I willing to pay for my comfort, and was it worth it?

I eventually found a perfectly imperfect resolution for smoking cessation. From my perspective, the method was practical for someone like me who'd exhausted all other alternatives. A few years ago, I found a small vaping vessel that doesn't produce a steam bomb like most standard-sized units.

The goal, of course, was to only breathe fresh air, so I'm not condoning, nor recommending anyone take my route. However, should someone decide to, it's important to do the homework first, because E-liquid products are not all created equal. The product I opted for was from a Canadian company that is one of the highest certified facilities in the country. The four ingredient non-fruity formulation uses vegetable glycerin which is food grade safe, it doesn't contain vitamin E acetate (a suspected culprit related to the recent spate of vaping deaths), nor does it contain anything related to popcorn lung.

Vaping has garnered a universally bad rap, on par with smoking cigarettes. I don't think vaping should be promoted in any way, shape, or form, but I used it as a stepping stone — a harm reduction tool. The chemical-laden, fruit-flavoured garbage produced from shady companies that targets and hooks young people should indeed be banned.

I'm also researching the use of cannabinoids, so if you see me looking a bit high while levitating, just flip me the peace sign and be on your way. I'll be doing just fine! My novel approach is daring to eat GF munchies during my mind's inaugural ballet performance!

Part Three

Every Tapestry Needs a Border

$\mathcal{V}.16$

"The most important thing in life is to stop saying 'I wish' and start saying 'I will.' Consider nothing impossible, then treat possibilities as probabilities."

~Charles Dickens

There's no need to imagine an existence blanketed in a threadbare rag. I have the tapestry. The undesired filaments representing deep inner conflict that were woven into its creation remain, but it still has the potential to be a masterpiece.

I've made much progress in sorting out the nuts and bolts for handling the various medical conditions; however, before beginning the completion of the border that will hold this tapestry together, a few straggling fragments need attention...

Enough precious time was squandered getting acclimated to the daunting task of scaling self-made mountains. These mountains, I'll admit, were crafted from nothing other than my very own special blend of fret fluff (a secret recipe I don't think you'll want).

When I wasn't busy building mountains, I'd continually seek some sort of Divine protection, a ritual that became my unique way of coping with anxiety. With no real calamities to cry over, my prayers were surely answered; however, I could no longer depend solely on angels. There was a risk that, having had enough of my excessive neediness, they'd decide to just come and get me.

There'd always be therapy (which I'd sensibly seek if need be), but I wished there was a more fitting way to handle a mind dancing the jitterbug, apart from depending on angels or cannabinoids to calm it. Doing so, seemed far less likely than spotting Peppy pig donning a purple tutu doing the splits at a pep rally.

Realistically, there could be no simple trick that would lead me to the solutions I was seeking: no group therapy in a sauna house located somewhere in the Himalayas, no hocus-pocus, no standing nude in the rain seeking guidance from spirits. However, it was apparent that great value could be found in discovering new tools to help.

A most useful tool was learning to superimpose pleasant images over negative ones, allowing my emotional reservoir to calmly idle in neutral, therefore keeping me ready to handle any unexpected calamity that might be thrown at me when strength was really needed. Even simple meditation made sense — making up a word with zero meaning and silently repeating it, as it wouldn't allow room for focusing on negative thoughts.

I'd need to throw caution to the wind and see if I could push myself in a new direction with the hope that I'd get a better result. Finally, I'd allow myself to believe that the blessedly simple life I'd built (as per my own blueprint), is the life I need to enjoy.

Talk is cheap though, because facing the epic collision of my countless contradictions felt like getting a much-needed bitch-slap from a wise angel. For example, I'd have to accept I'll always be worrying about damage caused by my years-long myopia around smoking, while, conversely, wanting to finally feel the overwhelming satisfaction that would come from clearing my headspace. Maybe I could make peace with patting myself on the back when I've achieved success, only to kick myself in the ass for my shortcomings.

Looking inward was also proving to be a productive use of my time when I turned my attention to insecurities. That seemingly imperfect heirloom tomato I almost left behind at the farmhouse aptly symbolized the analogy I was looking for — that we're all unique. Add in eccentricities; shyness; embarrassing neediness in social settings when food is involved; godawful confidence-deflating days when extra poundage, a bit of a chicken neck, or frizzy hair is exposed. All of this, and anything else I've failed to self-identify, shouldn't detract from my worth, unless I allow it to be that way.

Søren Keirkegaard summed things up nicely when he stated, *"People understand me so poorly that they don't even understand my complaint about them not understanding me."* That is true, but why does it matter? It doesn't, and this should've been obvious all along.

I'm finally able to admit that I've wilfully tried to adjust my Virgo's sapphire lens of perception in an attempt to make certain that all appears proper — minus, of course, any imperfections. Perhaps I'm more like Mother than I once realized. It's always been about the optics and a pinch of stubborn pride. But maybe, by being open and honest, I could tell the world, or even just one person, that there should be no shame for those of us who cart around a Mary Poppins bag that holds a few samples of imperfect humanness.

⌁

There was beauty in realizing that I might be a wee tad bit of a wreck, but I'm the lucky one — I'm here. Nothing yet is broken beyond repair. And, *I will* continue to focus on improving my circumstance by rejecting a life of self-imposed incarceration.

V.17

"Seize the moment. Remember all those women
on the Titanic who waved off the dessert cart."

~Erma Bombeck

Having the resolve to live a life free of self-incarceration meant I'd have to face a world beyond the boundaries of my comfort zone.

When we first discussed a trip to Europe, I worked extremely hard on throwing caution to the wind and seizing the moment, but the thought of following my GF diet while there still conjured up visions of the last rose being plucked from a prized rosebush, leaving nothing other than thorny branches. I'd need to appreciate, though, that there'd be no rose without the *beautiful strength of the branch*.

Even though my basic set of principles for traveling was set, things were a lot more complicated than simply passing up a bag of pretzels from the stewardess's cart. Honestly, my lifelong fantasy (before CD) was of jauntily eating my way through the experience with a napkin tied around my neck and fork in hand, but clearly there'd be a crimp in this scenario. There was no need to stop the world, allowing me to step off, but there was much to contemplate before going.

To encourage myself, I created a delightful, imaginary scene of arriving in Paris minus the emotional baggage. The only alternative crazy enough to be a decent distraction from the fear of making the trip would be trying to convert the sauerkraut in the fridge to whiskey. I'm sure you'd agree, using a tool to superimpose pleasant imagery was a much wiser strategy…

In my daydream, on the advice of friendly locals, Claude and I venture off the beaten path, which allows the luxury of avoiding tourist traps and being shuffled about like rowdy pigeons while angling for the perfect photo op. We see markets where generations of families hone their trade and love nothing more than to brag of their wares. Curious, engaging Claude finds himself taste-testing foods his new friend, *le marchand*, has given him to sample. Being wary of organs or anything with tentacles, I don't dare touch.

Meandering through ancient alleyways, we arrive at a cozy café where *le garçon*, another of Claude's instant new friends (this turns out to be true — he's a magnet for young European men who ask for selfies with him), graciously suggests a popular restaurant for dinner and offers to make our reservation. Upon his return, he tells us we should expect to be treated as royalty.

The restaurant's evening offerings are being prepared by methods steeped in tradition. It'll be food one can only dream about, if not in Paris. We opt for the cozy table in the corner, which is a little unevenly set due to the ancient wood-planked floors, but it's intimate and will do just fine. Le Monsieur suggests a grand *apéritif* to refresh us from the giddy tiredness that can only be felt when all of the senses have been teased, beyond even the best orgasmic climax.

Settled in, I pull out my dietary card, and we gesture for Monsieur. To show my deep respect and thinking he'll greatly appreciate my effort, my plan is to explain, with my limited French vocabulary, the issues with gluten and cross-contamination. Following the apéritif, we're now enjoying an excellent bottle of vintage wine, and, as my shyness begins to dissipate and fatigue washes over me, my impairment is such that all I can manage to utter is, *"Je suis fromage."*

Claude starts flailing his arms about, as is natural, and in his native Ontario French tongue, which isn't exactly Parisian French but regarded by some purists as a watered-down, off-script knock-off, explains that his wife is a "Glooten." Monsieur, confused as to why he was instructed to treat us as royalty when we don't appear to speak any discernible language, starts flailing his own arms.

Claude becomes oblivious to the ruckus before him as he slathers butter on each shred of broken bread. Monsieur has huffed off to see about a piece of *poulet* and steamed vegetables for me. I'm trying to look cheerful while pulling out a rice cracker from *je ne sais pas où* as I'm famished, having foolishly passed up the sample of blubbery delicacy earlier in the day.

While Claude is enjoying his appetizers, and knowing with all the fuss my dinner is at the bottom of the queue, I opt to leave him in blissful peace and head to the terrace.

In a quiet moment, there's clarity. I'm mesmerized by this place, adore this vintage wine, and — oh *Mon Dieu!* — how I love and worship Claude. And the irony isn't lost, when looking at my glass, that it appears *half full.*

It truly is all about perspective. And, if there's such a thing as reincarnation, maybe in my next life I'll opt to be a carefree little bird with a cozy, crumby nest, hidden in the crawling vines on the windowsill of a Paris boulangerie.

A wistful voice whispers from within, *"Eh bien, Colette, c'est la vie."*

V.18

"To be in hell is to drift; to be in heaven is to steer."

~George Bernhard Shaw

Undoubtedly, my absolute greatest joy would be the wonderful gift of finally being able to travel foot loose and fancy-free. With all previous flights, I'd have been far happier to be drugged, kenneled and stored in the underbelly of the plane — truly, in my mind, a more suitable arrangement.

Time and attitude had resolved my food debacles somewhat, and progress was being made dealing with insecurities, but, certainly, my fear of flying was a symptom that there were still lingering anxieties.

When we travelled to Hawaii we hop-scotched via Vancouver, which shortened the pain of a long flight, but nerve pills were needed. A helpful new little tool, sure, but one thing was certain: with the mind-bending awesomeness of the trip, the next long-haul excursion would demand full mental participation. I'd still want to have pills in my purse, but only to be used in case of emergency.

Daydreaming about travel was nice, but the time had

come to test my new resolve: learning to enjoy the journey (figuratively, and literally), not just the destination. This would be done by first examining the cold hard facts. Millions of people are flying daily, so statistically it's the safest way to go. I'm nothing more than a speck-on-the-flea-on-the-fly-on-the-wart-on-the-frog-on-the-log, and there's no reason to think that because I'm on the plane it's more likely to crash (unless, dear Lord, the aeronautic industry is pleasing shareholders by using the economically cheaper seal I developed for NASA, derived from my Black Forest cake recipe).

My mind was made up! I'd stop presuming small planes are nothing other than fancy canoes with wings. And, when on large planes, I'd no longer bruise Claude's knuckles on take-off. Instead, I'd focus on internal issues of the plane – like making sure the toilet seat remains upright when I'm hurriedly peeing like a racehorse so I can get back to the safety of my seat. Some people have joined the elite "Mile High Club," but I've spring-cleaned the lavatory, followed up by spot-washing my capris using a faucet that spouts water by the tablespoon (oh dear God, if ever there was a need for psychotherapy!) — a waiting lineup of curious but furious minds wondering, *what the hell?*

What the hell, and vafungula! Flap away, as the freest mountain bluebird. I'm good to go! There's no one better equipped than myself to steer my thoughts into positive territory. And, there's lots of exploring to be done to make up for lost time…

Our trip to Europe was a smashing success. My behaviour was stellar, allowing me to stay seated with the passengers, as no one suggested that it might be best to drug and cuff me. There's only a slim chance, should there be prolonged turbulence on future flights, that the need might arise to pilot the plane myself.

At the start of our journey we stayed in Eze, France, at the Chateau Eza. We had the Medieval Suite overlooking the Mediterranean, with a terrace large enough to host a busload of square dancers from Switzerland. We then traveled to Nice, staying at the renowned hotel Le Negresco, where we'd cross the street to walk along the ocean boardwalk on our jaunts to Old Nice. Several weeks after returning home, we heard that the Negresco lobby was used as a triage center following a terrorist attack, and our fond recollections of Nice were now deeply punctured with profound sadness. The images on television showed the heartfelt notes, teddy bears and candles that were left as memorials along a route now familiar. When the groovy doctor used thread to explain the fragility of life, he had it right.

From Nice, we headed to the stunning Principality of Monaco, where it's quite possible to believe that, for some, the road truly is paved in gold, witnessing, in awe, the over-indulgence that untold fortunes could afford.

Next, we were off to Tuscany, where the quintessential views of rolling fields of grape vines, bordered by narrow cypress trees, left me stunned and pinching myself to make sure the angels hadn't already come to take me home. I took pictures of "Nonna," her black dress peeking out from under her coat, with sickle in hand, hunched over and focused on her task. I wanted to tell her that I know her, that she's wise

"A beloved Nonna and her sickle" Tuscany, 2016

and kind, and no cook the world over could duplicate her recipes.

We got lost on our way to the B&B Casolare de Libbiano, and I was worried that our late arrival would be met with a little consternation, especially when coupled with the request for GF food. To our delight, we were greeted warmly, and a great dinner was prepared that started with the requisite cutting board of charcuterie and cheese. The owner's wife is the cook and she'd actually gone to the trouble to prepare a separate dinner for each of us. With the wine from their vineyard served in an iconic weaved twine decanter, white table linens crisply ironed, and everything else being antique but gleaming, the milieu was mesmerizing.

At the end of a long lane and mere feet from the entrance of the Casolare, ancient old houses, sheds, storage structures, and, shockingly, a large church, were clustered together. There was a swimming pool behind the main house and the vineyard beyond that. And, did I mention the church? Mamma Mia, it was the oddest sight one would ever see on a private family property. The walkways to the sides and front entrance had become covered with weed and grass, appearing as though no one had entered for many years. I wondered whether it might still be full of religious artifacts, and, why on earth was it closed up? To avoid unsettling the ghosts, who were undoubtedly cohabitating amongst the living, no queries were made. The owner told us the property had been owned by a family (unsure if he was related or a new owner) for over three hundred years, leaving one to assume this church, which gave the entire place a mystical feel, would have historical significance, possibly teeming with tragic, or at least unsettling, folklore.

The owner handed us a heavy iron key that needed to line up precisely with the groove notches in the antique keyhole if we had any intention of seeing our room. We were awestruck upon entering to see massive beams, some added as shims over time to prevent the ceiling from caving. Claude thought he'd been raised in an old farmhouse, but the buildings here were far older, and he could only marvel in disbelief at the elbow grease and ingenuity needed to maintain these ancient structures. Although I appreciated the furnishings, doilies and original artifacts (the paintings suited a property with an abandoned church but were a bit too dark and strange for my taste), there was still a small pang of uneasiness knowing that curious ghosts are always more active at night. Thankfully, as the images of the day rolled about in my mind, blissful sleep came easy.

In the morning, an older signor was on a tractor tending to the property, and with the window wide open, I stood in my nightgown inhaling the intoxicating smell of fresh cut grass, while the warm rays of sun enveloped the fledging grapes that were drenched from the overnight downpour. The spot where a spiritual connection might be made was found. This was the spot.

When the owner told us that they needed to prepare for supper and we should be back by eight p.m., it felt like Nonno had sternly, but lovingly, set the curfew to make sure we were home on time.

My disposition was never that of sour grapes, but I couldn't enjoy what my heart *really* yearned for while in Italy, which was the traditionally prepared gluten-laden manna from heaven that played the starring role throughout the course of my childhood in Toronto. When we left Tuscany to head back to France, a few moments alone were needed to settle in my mind and accept that reality with grace. Refocusing was all it took to see the bigger picture, and it was as fine a scene as one painted by Picasso himself.

In Paris, I revelled at the images of Parisian men and women riding the storied cliché of a vintage bike — of course, with proper posture — weaving through traffic perched on their seats like iconic French cats — over-confident, snooty looking, and not skittish in the least. They were impervious to the cacophony of congested chaos: neck scarves flapping in the wind, traditional dress attire, skinny-legged jeans, Burberry-like trench coats, bicycle baskets holding contrasting cargos of baguettes wrapped in brown paper or leather attaché cases.

Each *arrondissement* was unique and architecturally stunning. There were buildings with beautifully designed wrought-iron balconies — like suspended chariots ready to fly off on a whim. Adornments of gargoyles, angels, horses, beasts, busts, politicians, military figures, and figureheads were but a few of the infinite assortment of carvings and sculptures left as a testament to something historical, significant, grand or petite. They were beyond lovingly detailed — impossible to believe mere mortals had a hand in the production. This observation was true for all the ancient cities, villages and towns we visited in Europe. The people blessed to have been born to live in and around these buildings must have a daunting task preserving the stories that each structure begs to impart.

The memories will never be forgotten of sleeping at eclectic inns and grand hotels such as Il Casolare de Libbiano, Châteauneuf-Du-Pape (the dining and wine experience left me speechless), Castello Banfi — Il Borgo (ditto for this gem), Chateau Des Fines Roches, Cour des Loges, the Grand Hotel De Palais in Paris, and the B&B in Piazza within the ancient walls of San Gimignano.

Visiting Greece and Portugal was next on our bucket list.

Our dining experiences in the ancient Athens marketplace situated below the Parthenon of Athena were remarkable because eggplant dishes and fish were available on every menu, and there was little concern about food safety. The restaurants were open to the street, with tables appearing to have spilled out their doors, balancing precariously upright in the uneven, hilly and narrow passageways. Nothing felt touristy about the casual chaos of chatty, wine-drinking, chain-smoking Europeans, competing singers, and feral cats that were exceptionally well-mannered as they settled themselves at the best spot at our table, closest to the seafood. Claude's not a cat person, but he knew that he was the guest on their turf, and much to my surprise, he was quite content with the seating arrangements.

Our most memorable lunch was in the small town of Monchique in Portugal at the restaurant A. Charrette. Walking in, I had one of my "Oh. My. God!" moments. There were floor-to-ceiling wooden cabinets with glass doors on the far wall, filled with charming patterned china. From the kitchen doorway located behind the front counter, we could glimpse at the women cooking, and cooks in every sense of the word they were. Claude swooned when traditional dishes were brought to the table, surprisingly similar to those his mother prepared on the farm. The food was served as it would be at home, in large bowls to be shared. Cooked cabbage with new potatoes and vegetables mingled with different types of sausages in broth (he loved the blood sausage — me, too afraid to try). A dish of stewed pork from different parts of the animal (including cheek) appeared, also with vegetables, in broth. It was worth the sixty euros (cash only) it cost us to pay the *policia* for a bogus Sunday parking infraction. Along with two other couples nabbed in the sting, the spectacle provided entertainment for the gathering of old men drinking in the village square (just as I had long-ago pictured in my mind), which was located below the steep, ancient, stoned walkway leading to the restaurant. I would've washed our dirty lunch dishes and paid a ticket of six hundred euros for the experience.

To witness unbridled joy, you only need to give Claude a fresh garden tomato, cucumber or green onion. No recipe required — just add salt. He remembers his uncle showing up at the farm each year in late summer with his car full of turnips, and I don't know if his mother served them at every meal to avoid wasting them, but it's the only vegetable he seems satisfied to set aside. The reward from toiling with earth — the smell, the touch, the taste, even the aches — have formed Claude's perception of food.

I skipped along through life avoiding cracks in concrete sidewalks adorned with spit stains and dried gum wads, which made it somewhat surprising to find myself falling head over heels in love with the province of Newfoundland & Labrador.

I expected to appreciate its beautiful ruggedness, but never expected to have my heart filled with love for the island people, who are deeply rooted in this place — they are indomitable, fearless of strangers, vocal with praise for respect shown to their home, and incredibly spirited in nature.

As part of our stay at Fogo Island Inn, the staff arranged to have a local pick us up to explore. I was reluctant to take advantage of the perk but was soon completely smitten with our guide Helen. As we drove, we saw landscape that was dotted with battered boats, long ago docked on dry land, and water-logged sea legs that could barely hold the weight of iconic stages used for drying and salting the fishermen's catch. Her private, lonely garden was located in a communal field perched on the ocean's edge, dilapidated wooden fences dividing her plot from the others. It was a beautiful spot, but it was hauntingly sad to see the abandoned overgrowth of the other gardens — tangles of wild grasses and stubby shrubs. They struggled against the imposing wind, almost purposely willing me to ponder over the hardships that have impacted the island people — the collapse of livelihoods from depleted cod stocks — their storied way of life forever altered. (Rebounding cod stocks are still in a critically fragile state.)

Helen gifted me the last of the carrots that were probably happy to be of service and eaten, the alternative being to shrivel up and die before the arrival of snow. I was deeply touched. Claude would have a lifetime of memories, sharing similar experiences of rural life with Helen, and I would have "one" — but a most spectacular one. Perhaps, a few motherly spirits have followed me home, which might be the only explanation for my continued fascination with the place.

A completely unrelated but funny anecdote highlights Helen's and Claude's unpretentious nature. Claude had slipped and missed a wooden slat on a small bridge, his foot sinking into the murky wet mud. He hung the sock on the exterior of his rolled-up window and we drove away with it flopping about in the wind. I sat in the back seat watching them roar like hell with laughter. Think of how many places you could do this, and not look silly!

The inn experience perfectly showcased the intricacies, eccentricities, and colourful nature of this mystical place. Our room, with its floor-to-ceiling windows, provided a stunning, unobstructed ocean view, and I could feel an indescribable sense of soothing solitude. The high vaulted ceilings made the room feel large and airy, but having an actual wood-burning stove made it also feel cozy and cocoon-like. Much of what is contained within the inn has been lovingly designed with local input and handcrafted by local producers. Women, following tradition, have sewn or hand-hooked the unique and colourful comforters, furniture cushions, rugs, decorative pillows, and tapestries.

The food (served by warm-hearted islanders) was abundant, locally sourced, and soul-satisfyingly delicious. The creatively fresh entrees weren't presented in an overly fussy manner, which meant the down-home roots of the recipes never got lost in translation. On the morning we left, the baker had gifted me with two loaves of GF bread, sandwiches for Claude, and sweets and drinks to have on our ferry ride. Now that's how you say goodbye to a friend with CD who might have trouble finding GF options on the journey ahead!

Fogo Island Inn has been built by, and for, the island people. Innkeeper Zita Cobb and the Shorefast Foundation, a registered charity, ensure that the people of Fogo and Change Islands are the sole benefactors, and it's my sincerest wish for their continued success.

It was suggested we visit the charmingly picturesque Change Islands. When I called Beulah Oakes, the owner of Seven Oakes Island Inn and Cottages, she told me the inn (a refurbished fish merchant house circa the 1800s) was now closed for the season. The linens she'd stripped from beds in the cottages, located below the main house on the oceanfront, were still slightly damp, and were now draped over the furniture in the front parlour. Regrettably, the time had come to sell the inn, she explained, as her husband had passed away in recent years and the work was becoming too burdensome to handle on her own. If you understand the nature of a Newfoundlander, there's no need for me to explain how it came to pass that, by the time we ended our lengthy call, conversing like old friends, she insisted we not dilly-dally getting on the next ferry, and we'd be having cod for dinner. She'd received a call earlier in the day from two girls who were also late-season travellers hoping to stay, and decided, in a heartbeat or less, that one more night's company might just do her good. We'll always be thankful for her decision.

The house is perched at the top of a rocky mount, and when we arrived Beulah had the last of her loads of laundry on the clothesline, not an easy mode for drying things when fall days get shorter and warm breezes quickly turn cool in late afternoon. As I stood on the porch in awe of the view, familial roots were stirring from beneath me — and yet, we were complete strangers before arrival, or so I thought. Many Irish families started Canadian life after landing on the shores here, which I'd gander to say must have included my Sullivan descendants. To the right, a bit over yonder, the timeworn-whitewashed church stood with its regal steeple, and weather-beaten chalky-white tombstones smudged with moss seemed willed by the dead to stay upright. And, straight ahead, the sun, cruelly teasing a few glimmers of light before descending into slumber, didn't fool the ocean — it shuddered as if suddenly chilled, the white-tipped rolling waves in assorted hues of blue, lulling the fish to sleep.

The dining room was a trove of personal treasures, each with a story belonging to this particular place, exclusively. The dinner was served on fine china, noted for its European origin. It was mighty tempting to snatch a chunk of the bread Claude was relishing, but I instead stayed focused on the cod, so fresh that if it were not for being cooked, one would wonder if the fish here were trained to jump out of the water and onto the plate. Beulah stated that she never once purchased store-bought bread or dessert, making it fresh every day from scratch. This incredible woman, being the pilot at the helm, had her manual memorized, to be sure.

The girls had left early the following morning, but we found ourselves lingering. While I was showering and packing, Beulah sat with her coffee and reminisced with Claude, which is one of his most cherished pastimes. She didn't appear to be in a rush to get to her final chores. The yet-to-be told stories of Beulah's new beginning lay ahead, but in this story, we felt extraordinarily blessed to be written into the last chapter of her final hours of stewardship of Seven Oakes Island Inn.

At this point we've boarded planes for many destinations, a statement which some seasoned travellers might balk at because we've barely scratched the moss on the surface of a travel log, let alone the log itself. Sure, but there's no longer a need for me to pretend that watching reruns of the late chef Anthony Bourdain's travel shows is a sufficient way to enjoy the world. After surviving the first couple of trips, the thought of going on the next one was beyond exciting, and you'd think the house was on fire when the suitcases were packed. Each time I was rushing off to save myself — while finding myself at the same time.

Travelling has pushed me beyond my comfort zone countless times, and as terrifying in the moment as some experiences have been, I've come to accept the idea that if my departure ticket is already dated, there's nothing to gain sitting at home worrying about it.

Trekking the 10k Joffre Mountain pass in British Columbia to see mind-blowing mountain lakes of blue-green glacier water was unimaginable a few short years ago. Discovering a place where supernatural, dead silence exists, far above the earth on an open ski lift; or sobbing in fear while driving through clouds to reach the magical summit of Haleakalã; or praying when driving through treacherous cliffside passages into remote rainforest areas, and then surprised to come upon a lean-to where we'd drink coffee ground from locally grown beans or sip coconut water right out of the fruit – all of these experiences have made my life richer.

There's just no going back to the darkness of a mind closet where old ghosts of angst can easily grasp me if I get too close.

"Never too old to go on a famiy foursome getaway"
Kristina Walkling & Kris Ledoux, Santa Monica CA, 2018

$\mathcal{V}.19$

"I thought yesterday was the first day of the rest of my life but it turns out today is."

~Steve Martin

I'm a clueless amateur, but I'm finally at peace enjoying the art of self-expression. Finding a creative outlet as an alternative to being the lead dancer in Swan Lake wasn't exactly a straightforward hike, but I'm happy just the same.

I'm not quite sure what the hell I was thinking, years ago, when I went a bit overboard with the novel idea of trying to connect with spirits. I'd read about a guy who could only paint stick people until he started channeling his energy towards famous dead art masters. His cosmic experiment was a smashing success, and he started producing works of art eerily similar to great masterpieces.

Hope and inspiration washed over me, and I knew I'd found my true calling. A spirit wanting to use me as a vessel had better take a number and get queued up; the waiting line was going to be long. In a state of frenzy to emulate the man I'd read about, and having no idea what technique to use, I thought it logical to extend my invitation to the spirits by piously looking upward with raised arms.

"My dear, what lofty ambitions," I muttered.

I was confident I could rely solely on Divine intervention until a professional artist warned me it's difficult to achieve success without using a picture as a point of reference. With this news, things were beginning to look somewhat complicated, and I was in a bit of a pickle. A reference requires focus, but my plan was to paint in a trance-like state of semi-conscious relaxation.

Believe me I was ready, having invested in the easel, the finest of brushes, cute little doodads fashioned like miniature trowels, all sorts of jars I was clueless what to do with but was sure would be found in a master's paint box, and enough little tubes of paint to change the colour of the stripes on a herd of zebras.

As I worked with the potential Renoir replica, the paintbrush guided me — at other times, it was the other way around. The prospect of what might be revealed was exhilarating. But after I put in hours of intense work, managing to distribute the paint equally between the canvas and my sweatshirt (which was smartly used to wipe my brushes), despair began creeping in, sweeping aside any hope of achieving my perceived calling.

Warring sides of my personality were the crux of the problem. The sensible, obedient part of me tried hard to adhere to the required conformity. This side clashed with the untameable, exuberant side of me, maybe a little intoxicated from the heavenly, heady scent of oil and Varsol and maybe a little over-the-moon giddy with the prospect of a spiritual experience.

I'd been alone all along.

The short-sighted spirits had foolishly ignored my golden invitation, and that tidbit of professional advice was harder to apply than learning to speak Mandarin using an Asian restaurant's take-out menu.

The reference picture's ocean morphed into forest, cherubic children turned into leafy shrubs, waves became a swampy road leading to nowhere, and the pale blue sky grew darker and more foreboding with each coat of paint.

Drained of creative juice, I stood in amazement at the oily mess. I'd have to accept that being off course from the reference picture proved my lack of talent, and where to set up my permanent art studio would never be a pressing problem.

I let frustration deflate me, and then allowed self-pity to defeat me. My passion for painting was gone. Years slipped by, vanishing into thin air. The paint dried up in the tubes.

Why the hell would I only settle on a Renoir replica, or nothing at all? It's because I foolishly thought there was all the time in the world to waste. But I'm a little wiser now, and each precious moment must count, so the paint supplies have been restocked. I marvel at how durable canvas is when a tree is painted in, scraped out of the scene, and repainted, several times over. I've no need to allow any painting of mine to mutate into something best suited for storage in a closet, a spot where those now bored ghosts (I'll no longer be their muse) might signal their disapproval of the new decor. As I focus on my project, the old-new, upside-down, facts-are-fiction world somehow seems to carry on without my watchful eye.

An abundance of love buoys me, and my desire to move forward is undisputable. But I'm always mindful that undercurrents of irrational thought can trigger a tsunami, and I won't be cured of anything. Thankfully, though, I'm not yet scavenging for discarded remnants of "this and that," which might do the trick in a pinch if I were building a bird's nest: Instead, I'm focused on the journey. It's a journey which, at this point in my life, is just as valuable as any unknown destination.

This battered slate roof is a tad bit high for my liking, but when I shift from side to side, I like the sound of the rat-tat-tat on the tile. There's no need to worry that I'll fall off because my fine, feathery flaps, in sapphire blue, are securely woven into place. I can go higher if I want to or slowly glide downward towards the cobblestoned street.

It's a glorious morning, but my preference is to wait until evening for my downward venture when the *sloppy indulgers,* as I like to call them, have gone home. All are just too anxious to gorge on their baguette when exiting the boulangerie, not waiting to open their *beau cadeau* until seated on the bench in the park. I'm not cross with the mess they leave behind, because their loss, the finest of crumbs, will be my gain.

The tops of stately trees are visible, their leaves tinged orange and red, flushed from shivering all night to stay warm. I need to squint now, but in the distance, the shimmering threads of a weathered, second-hand, but resplendent, tapestry is coming into view. Madame is setting it out to freshen in the crisp September air.

Oh Mon Dieu, c'est incroyable! It appears the journey is endless.

"Reach high, for stars lie hidden in you. Dream deep, for every dream precedes the goal."

~Rabindranath Tagore

Maybe you know me a little better. Maybe I know myself a little better. Maybe you don't — and maybe I don't. It's okay either way.

There's only one *me* — thank God for lucky stars.

There's only one *you* — that's why God made stars.

Priceless originals, we are.

My goal was to tell my story. Dream deep and reach high if your goal is to tell yours — by writing, singing, dancing, or painting it — or whispering it to the wind.

Much love,

Colette

A Few More Words

"Quotations are a columnist's bullpen. Stealing someone else's words frequently spares the embarrassment of eating your own."

~Peter Anderson

It's seems ironic to me that I'm ending my story by using a quote to explain my use of quotes. I decided to incorporate them into my story because a few simple words can convey a mighty powerful message. I love quotes. Our lives are richer because of sage words from teachers, writers, poets, songwriters, philosophers, humanists, comedians, and the odd bartender. Their words can enlighten us, bring comfort, provide guidance, and help strengthen our resolve when weakness and weariness set in.

This book is my first attempt at writing, and I'm pretty happy I managed to get it finished. One of my biggest concerns was writing about the medical aspect of CD and my highly embarrassing personal issues, convinced that the dry text needed to provide accurate information wouldn't make for good reading.

At one point, I tried sprucing things up by creating imaginary stories into which to insert the information. In one scene I had Sean Spicer, Trump's former Press Secretary, hiding in a bush with a rogue elf from the North Pole smoking

Marlboros, while in another scene, I had him in the elf sleigh used in the Elf movie. In an earlier scene written years ago, I had an Italian organ grinder, with his sidekick monkey, who hung around for so long in the text that he thought he'd made the cut. Then I said *vafungula,* and only allowed the elves from the North Pole to stay because, after all, they were busy gluing Christmas toys.

Thinking I could "simply" sit down and produce a book was absolute nonsense. The truth is, good God, I've got lists: lists about the lists; templates; notes on principles; grids; rough copies that I thought were final; and final copies that ended up being rough; and, about a thousand versions of the manuscript that I smartly labeled "Fuck, Don't Lose," because I never save things properly, nor properly retrieve things that are saved.

With the first draft of the manuscript, it looked like I was assembling a Plumbers Manual. Help in organizing it was, however, on the way. I'm more than thankful that the stars lined up, and the late Beverly Swerling, a renowned American writer of historical fiction, assessed the manuscript and provided me with much-needed direction. Her report, as I feared, was critical. Basically, I'd have to go back to square one and start over — again, and again, and again. Putting aside Beverly's critical assessment of structural flaws (at one point I tried to convince her that the manuscript was in such good shape, a toss in a bingo drum couldn't mess it up – she thought otherwise), I was still tickled pink when she stated she could see the "genius" in my writing. However, when I recently reread her note, she'd actually stated my writing was "genuine." I'm thankful for my hilarious misreading, because that one word propelled me forward. Who the hell thinks words don't matter? I'm still roaring with laughter!

To my wonderful son-in-law Christopher Walkling, a big thank you! I know you've tried teaching me what is considered basic computer knowledge, and I've been a most unruly student, but do know it was greatly appreciated. You claim that I've done things with a computer you've never seen before, and, given your highly skilled work in the field of education and technology, I know you're right. I'll understand fully, my lovebug, if you enter into a witness protection program should I pronounce the start of a second book.

Denise (Lamirande), you've been with me from the start — this journey through life with you was a gift bestowed upon me by fate, and I'm more than grateful. Thanks for your help with this project. Lynn (Elliot), I'm grateful for you too, with a special nod for undertaking the daunting task of reading the worst draft of all — the very first one. Leanne Selevich, my wonderful niece, I hope you know how much I've appreciated having you as my go-to proofreader. Keith Selevich — artist and graphic designer extraordinaire — thank you for your earnest interest in this project. Emily Hong, a special thanks for always being so good to me. I'll never forget that it was your words of encouragement that prompted me to set up my easel, and I'll always be grateful.

To: Cyndy Lawrence, my one and only Lambchop, my first friend Marie Jackson (always remembered as Pia Iannace), Annette Ledoux, Diane Deschamps, Urgel Ledoux, Peggy and Gilles Ledoux, Natasha and Mitch Merante, Lorna Walkling, Sarah Innes, Karen Chamberlain, Mary (Ferretti) MacKinnon, Lori Mayne, Susan Harwood, Sharon Warnick, Mark Meilleur, Maureen Landers, Anne Moffat, Grace Fowler, George and Jason Lamirande, Dustin Magill, Mariah and Mark Sajatovic, Jordan Ringuette, Jennifer, Jessica, and Brenda Hong, and Marion Parish, cousins Maureen Ross Miller, Nancy Campbell, Kevin Ross, and Normand Bertrand, with special mention to book contributor Chef Andrew Bridgman, and niece Lise Bridgman — Thanks for your friendship, your words of encouragement, your recipes, or reading any version of my "vomit drafts."

A special note of thanks to Dr. Margaret Paul, surgeon, Dr. Alan Aylett, GP, and Dr. Scott Shulman, gastroenterologist, for the years of being tucked under your wings. I'm also beyond grateful for the exceptional care from Dr. Michael Ford, and Dr. Joel Finkelstein, orthopaedic surgeons. And, a note of thanks to Candace Morison, TuiNa; Dr. of Homeopathy, Reflexology; Nutritionist, for your keen intuitive skill and friendship extended to our family.

Dr. Katarzyna Lukomska and Walter Sitkowski, thank you for sending Margaret Moore to me, although I suspect she was flown in on the wings of an angel. Dr. Lukomska, we truly feel blessed for your exemplary care, and your razor-sharp diagnostic ability. The time we've been blessed to spend with you and Walter will always be cherished.

Margaret, you've edited so many "final" drafts I'm sure you've lost count. You've been my lifeline during the writing process, and there's *a thread belonging to you (and only you) woven into my tapestry*. I simply could not have enjoyed, nor endured, this project without you. Tom (Moore), you're the cat's meow, and I'm sending thanks for allowing me to wife-nap your sidekick. Marg, my friend, I love you dearly.

As I move forward, I'd like to extend thanks to Shanda Trofe at Transcendent Publishing, for reading the manuscript and encouraging me to publish. Dana Micheli, editor, thank you! You've been able to calm my jitters and have had the patience and sense of humour needed to handle my nuttiness.

Gosh, I'm beginning to sound like I'm accepting an award, so…

"I'd like to thank the Academy; the producer of my imaginary movie starring Sean Spicer; anyone I've missed acknowledging, with sincerest apologies; and Mother, who, if she's read any of this cosmically, might greet me at the Pearly Gates of heaven with a good quality cast iron frying pan, with no intention of using it for one of my recipes!

Dorval Ledoux, just as I was wrapping up this project, you embarked on quite the journey. Your spirituality, spectacular sense of humour, and determination to overcome, against all odds, have been simply stunning to watch. As a family, we're honoured that you've allowed us to enlist as your pit crew while you endure this trek. You've shown us what bravery looks like. My love, I'll always have your "Go-Go" juice or dinner ready, and Claude will always be ready for a road trip that might just lead to a pot of gold — or maybe just pot! And, by the way, the pigeon is gone! You and Claude convinced me it had to "flock off."

"Aging like fine wine" "COVID coiffed Claude"
Walkling Cottage on Jack Lake, 2020
Photo credit: Chris Walkling

Claude, my love, you're my absolute everything, and I'll love you for eternity. You've given me more support than I've ever deserved. If I were a little teapot, short and stout, you'd be the sturdy handle and much needed spout. No more words are needed.

Kristina and Kristopher, what use would we have had for a teapot without the teacups? *The two of you completed the set. We will love you for always and forever.*

Poun and Me-Bobbidy/Buddy, I hope this writing endeavour will not cause too much embarrassment! I'm never at a loss for words, but I just can't seem to find any that will convey what needs to be said, so I'll keep it simple. Instinctively, your lives are purpose-driven. There are your countless acts of compassion and outreach to others, which you don't seek credit for because it's never about optics or self-praise. It's about decency; it's your unwavering commitment to family; it's your attention to the environment, which shines through *brightly* Kris, in your work with GOTG (Go Off The Grid); it's being givers and not takers. All of these, and countless other attributes, make claiming you as my own my proudest achievement. Time well spent is being together. Set a communal table, even if you're only having hotdogs. Dad says don't forget the tablecloth (white) and candles (lots). He won't be thrilled with the idea of serving hotdogs (I've spoiled him rotten), so perhaps use some of my recipes instead. Most importantly — *Always consider that every bad day is good, every good day is a gift, every great day should be dedicated to memory and recalled when a frown needs to be turned upside down. I'll never leave either of you, or my grandkids, even when I leave.* (Don't worry! I don't plan on writing poetry!)

As for the angels, it's a question of faith. Much like the dilemma as to what came first, the chicken or the egg, the answer that rings true to *me* is all that matters. I've asked for proof of Your existence and you have answered — Keira and Noah are fine examples. I am thankful.

Personal Observations

"What is important is to spread confusion, not eliminate it."

~Salvador Dalí

I still have unanswered questions with regard to the GF movement, and I think they're worthy of consideration when discussing gluten-related issues…

Yes, gluten is my kryptonite, but what is it to someone who doesn't have my oddball condition? It baffles me to see hordes of people eschewing wheat and/or gluten. Many of them, like frustrated sleuths, are trying to find the best way to understand, and then validate, their issues. My fate has been sealed, but I'm still perplexed that, seemingly overnight, millions of people have woken up with gut-related symptoms. Something's going on, but what?

I've threaded together a rudimentary list which highlights, strictly from a personal standpoint, a few of the more fascinating and confusing aspects of the debate surrounding the ingestion of wheat and/or gluten.

1. Will health benefits of a GF diet be proven for the general population? Are people converting to GF, perhaps prematurely, without diagnosis, thus complicating finding the answer, because the proverbial cart is being put ahead of the horse?

Countless GF processed products are sub-standard — less fibre — non-fortified — more sugar — and yet people are converting, thinking it's a healthier choice. It's stunning to see the market growth in GF products, when, in reality, the vast majority of the population has yet to be diagnosed with any identifiable condition related to gluten.

Seeing the explosion in availability of GF essentials on grocery store shelves has been exhilarating. But undoubtedly, most of the industry's multi-billion-dollar profit will come from convenience foods that will overshadow the very essence of what was actually healthy about the GF diet, which was until recently, *a gaping lack in availability of unnecessary, processed Frankenfood.*

Exploiting GF alternative grains by churning out calorie-dense, saturated/trans-fat-laden, nutrient-deficient, sugar-packed, chemical-coated-screwed-up-piles-of-junk, equal to what's been done with wheat grain, seems dangerously short-sighted at best.

2. Next, I want to understand if there's merit to the controversial argument that we should not consume wheat (not just gluten but the grain itself).

If you're looking for an argument against eating wheat, Dr. William Davis wrote a book called *Wheat Belly*, which many people credit for improving their life. His book, in part, contributed to propelling the GF movement forward.

An excerpt from an article titled, "The Dangers of Going Gluten Free," written by Cathy Gulli, looks at the assertions made in the book:

"The irony, however, is that William Davis detests his new-found role as poster boy for the gluten-free food industry—and actually discourages people from buying these products because of

their low nutritional value. 'This has nothing to do with gluten,' he tells Maclean's. Instead, he takes issue with how wheat has been grown, and altered through hybridizations over the last several decades, which he believes is harmful to human health. 'If we view wheat as nothing more than a vehicle for gluten, we are not going to understand all the issues that are important about modern wheat.'"

Gulli also explains the perspective of Ravindra Chibbar, Canada research chair in crop quality and Professor at University of Saskatchewan, who argues against Dr. Davis's wheat assessment:

"It's a highly inflammatory view, and crop experts such as Chibbar insist it is without merit. Hybridization means 'you take one plant that has a feature you like, you cross it with another one and you get a progeny that has characteristics that you want,' he explains. 'It has been going on for tens of thousands of years. It happens with all the crops, it's not just wheat.'" [viii]

3. And finally, I want to understand the argument that questions whether increased use of extracted gluten from wheat has had an adverse effect on our health.

(Note: "Vital gluten" refers to gluten extracted from wheat in its pure form, which is then added to a wide variety of commercial food product applications.)

Below is an excerpt from "Is Gluten Content to Blame for the Rise in Celiac Disease," an article written by Patrick Bennett:

"'Gluten,' explains Donald Kasarda, a PhD collaborator with the U.S. Department of Agriculture, 'tends to take up between 70 and 75 percent of wheat's total protein content. Thus, if the overall protein levels have remained steady, so has the amount of gluten. If there has indeed been an increase in celiac disease

during the latter half of the century, wheat breeding for higher gluten content does not seem to be the basis.'

*... 'Based on the data he has studied, he estimates that between 1977 and today, **vital gluten** consumption in the United States has tripled. He notes this time period is the same as the estimated rise in celiac disease, but whether this has to do with the development of celiac disease remains to be determined.'"* [ix]

Researchers have a lot on their plate and, as you can clearly see, opinions differ. If an evolutionary change in wheat or over-exposure to gluten causes greater intolerance or disease, perhaps in the not too distant future guidelines for consumption will carry a caveat for the entire population.

The pros and cons of the GF movement are numerous. On one hand, it's brought awareness of CD, but on the other, the fad element (maybe unfairly described as we await answers) has had some detrimental consequences.

As I've noted, it was baffling, but also shocking, to watch the GF movement explode before my eyes. It felt personal – dealing with the jokes, the naysayers, and eye-rollers, all oblivious to the dire predicament that comes with an official diagnosis. Comedians had a field day adding to their joke repertoire, and billboards advertised GF haircuts, water, or oil lubes.

Unfortunately, the damage caused by dismissing *any* gluten issue as frivolous is a serious matter. Let me tell you, bashing the GF diet is considered pretty "tasteless" from the perspective of many in the celiac community. Parents with young kids living with CD, in particular, are finding it much more difficult to keep their children unharmed due to ill-informed attitudes, and this is truly shameful. Those who are properly diagnosed may be as hard to identify as "the celiac needle in a haystack," but this is why awareness, with emphasis on the disease aspect, is so important.

Now, on a lighter note, the one person who could do "gluten" jokes that were actually funny was the late John Pinette (Goggle his stand-up routines). "Have you tried gluten-free bread? It needs gluten. I don't know what gluten is, but apparently, it's delicious."

Glossary

Celiac Disease

Canadian Celiac Association: [x]

"Celiac disease is a medical condition in which the absorptive surface of the small intestine is damaged by a protein called gluten. This results in an inability of the body to absorb nutrients: protein, fat, carbohydrates, vitamins and minerals, which are necessary for good health. Although statistics are not readily available, it is estimated that 1 in 133 persons in North America are affected by celiac disease."

"A wide range of symptoms may be present. Symptoms may appear together or singularly in children or adults. In general, the symptoms of untreated celiac disease indicate the presence of malabsorption due to the damaged small intestine."

The University of Chicago, Celiac Disease Center: www.cureceliacdisease.org

Excerpts regarding CD symptoms: *"There are more than 200 signs and symptoms of celiac disease, yet a significant percentage of people with celiac disease have no symptoms at all. The undamaged part of their small intestine is able to absorb enough nutrients to prevent symptoms. However, people without symptoms are still at risk for some of the complications of celiac disease." "Children tend to have the more classic signs of celiac disease, including growth problems (failure to thrive), chronic diarrhea/constipation, recurring abdominal bloating and pain, fatigue and irritability."*

Gluten Intolerance (NON-CELIAC Gluten Sensitivity – NCGS)

Excerpt from an article written by Lee Marshall, entitled, "Gluten-free not just a fad for some." [xi]

"Dr. Mohsin Rashid, a gastroenterologist at the IWK Health Centre in Halifax, says that non-celiac gluten-sensitivity is a newly coined phenomenon. 'We don't know exactly what happens. We're just trying to probe the surface of this issue.'

What doctors do know is that people with non-celiac gluten-sensitivity have celiac-like gastrointestinal and neurological side-effects but no autoimmune reaction to gluten. There is no way to diagnosis sensitivity: the blood tests and biopsy for celiac disease come back negative.

But some researchers think non-celiac gluten-sensitivity may be more prevalent than celiac disease and that the prevalence may be increasing at a faster rate."

Gluten

Gluten is composed of two different proteins: gliadin and glutelin. It is found in grains such as wheat, rye, barley, and triticale, and gives dough its elastic texture.

Calculation of Gluten Content in Food

Excerpt from a CCA article explaining how gluten content in food is calculated: [xii]

"20 ppm

The term 'parts per million' is used regularly when we talk about gluten free products, but what does it really mean?

Parts per million, or ppm, is a ratio that indicates 1 unit of the item of interest in a total of 1 million units.

Using a ratio like parts per million works well as a general description because it doesn't matter whether you are describing the amount of gluten in a liquid or in a solid food.

When we talk about total gluten intake, though, we need to convert the ratio to a specific quantity. 20 ppm means 20 milligrams of gluten in 1,000,000 milligrams of food.

To make this more concrete, a slice of regular wheat bread might contain 4 grams of gluten. If you eat gluten-free bread containing the maximum level 20 ppm of gluten, it would take 200 kilograms of food to match the 4 grams of gluten in a single piece of bread."

Villi

Mayo Clinic: [xiii]

"When the body's immune system overreacts to gluten in food, the immune reaction damages the tiny, hair-like projections (villi) that line the small intestine. Villi absorb vitamins, minerals and other nutrients from the food you eat. Normally, villi resemble the deep

pile of a plush carpet, on a microscopic scale. The damage resulting from celiac disease makes the inner surface of the small intestine appear more like a tile floor. As a result, your body is unable to absorb nutrients necessary for health and growth."

Microscopic Colitis – (MC)

Mayo Clinic: [xiv]

"Microscopic colitis is an inflammation of the large intestine (colon) that causes persistent watery diarrhea. The disorder gets its name from the fact that it's necessary to examine colon tissue under a microscope to identify it.

There are two types of microscopic colitis:

Collagenous colitis, in which a thick layer of protein (collagen) develops in colon tissue

Lymphocytic colitis, in which white blood cells (lymphocytes) increase in colon tissue

It's not clear what causes the inflammation of the colon found in microscopic colitis. Researchers believe that the causes may include:

Medications that can irritate the lining of the colon

Bacteria that produce toxins that irritate the lining of the colon

Viruses that trigger inflammation

Immune system problems, such as rheumatoid arthritis or celiac disease, that occurs when your body's immune system attacks healthy tissues."

Glycemic Index

Below is an excerpt from the Mayo clinic regarding the glycemic index. It gives a few key reasons why one might consider eating foods with a *low* GI: [xv]

"Purpose: Diets based on the glycemic index suggest that you eat foods and beverages with low glycemic index rankings to help you keep your blood sugar balanced. Proponents say this will help you lose weight and reduce risk factors for certain chronic diseases.

Why you might follow the glycemic index diet:

Want to change blood sugar imbalances related to your current diet

Want to change your overall eating habits

Don't want to count calories or go low-carb

Want a diet that you can stick to for the long term

Check with your doctor or health care provider before starting any weight-loss diet, especially if you have any health conditions, including diabetes.

Foods ranked by the glycemic index are given scores:

High: 70 and up. Examples include instant white rice, brown rice, plain white bread, white skinless baked potato, boiled red potatoes with skin and watermelon.

Medium: 56 to 69. Examples include sweet corn, bananas, raw pineapple, raisins and certain types of ice cream.

Low: 55 and under. Examples include raw carrots, peanuts, raw apple, grapefruit, peas, skim milk, kidney beans and lentils."

Garlic

I've always cooked with a lot of garlic, but a recent study merits some attention. I've decided that more raw garlic has to be incorporated into my eating plan. The olives stuffed with garlic that I eat are pickled, and I didn't know if pickling alters the "raw" status of garlic, so I spoke to my local pharmacist. He believes the acid component to pickling might alter the garlic, so if the study states to eat it raw, you're best to do just that.

Here is an excerpt from a fascinating article from CBC News:

"Eating Raw Garlic Can Prevent Cancer, Study Suggests.

Eating raw garlic twice a week can cut the chances of lung cancer by almost half, new research suggests.

The results, published online in the journal Cancer Prevention Research, showed those who ate raw garlic at least twice a week cut the risk of lung cancer by 44 per cent, even if they were exposed to high-temperature cooking-oil fumes, which is thought to be another trigger for the disease.

The herb even reduces the risk in smokers by 30 per cent, the research suggested.

Scientists at the Jiangsu Provincial Centre for Disease Control and Prevention carried out face-to-face interviews with 1,424 lung cancer patients with 4,500 healthy adults in China from 2003 to 2010.

Each one was questioned on their dietary and lifestyle habits, including how often they consumed garlic and whether they smoked.

The key ingredient appears to be a chemical called allicin, released when the clove is crushed or chopped. Allicin is believed to reduce inflammation in the body and act as an antioxidant, reducing damage from so-called radicals to the body's cells.

It's not clear whether cooked garlic has the same effect.

In a report on their findings the researchers said: 'Garlic may potentially serve as a preventive agent for lung cancer.'" [xvi]

Olives & Olive Oil

The health benefits of olives and olive oils have been cited in numerous publications, and the results are stunning. There are far too many benefits to list here, but they range from minimized cancer risk to reduced high blood pressure and reduced incidence of diabetes. Olive oil is known to help tackle the underlying causes of Metabolic Syndrome.

The excerpts below are from an article titled "The Mediterranean Diet and Metabolic Syndrome," written by Elena Paravantes:

> *"Pothoulakis explains that the metabolic syndrome is a combination of abdominal obesity, high blood pressure, abnormal cholesterol, and high blood sugar."*

> *"Metabolic syndrome is connected to the obesity epidemic of our time, a big belly poisons our metabolism, and a poisoned metabolism can result in type 2 diabetes, heart attacks, stroke, or sudden death."*[xvii]

Blue Baby – Rh Factor (Taken from standfordchildrens.org)

Key points about Rh disease

- Rh disease occurs during pregnancy. It happens when the Rh factors in the mom's and baby's blood don't match.

- If the Rh-negative mother has been sensitized to Rh-positive blood, her immune system will make antibodies to attack her baby.

- When the antibodies enter your baby's bloodstream, they will attack the red blood cells. This causes them to break down. This can lead to problems.

- This condition can be prevented. Women who are Rh-negative and haven't been sensitized can receive medicine. This medicine can stop their antibodies from reacting to the baby's Rh-positive cells.

Suggested Resources for CD Guidance:

As far as managing my diet, I always go to reliable resources — Shelley Case, RD, Celiac Nutrition Expert, Author, Speaker, President of Case Nutrition Consulting Inc; Canadian Celiac Association; Dr. Stefano Guandalini, The University of Chicago, Celiac Disease Center; Dr. Alessio Fasano, Director of the Center for Celiac Research at Massachusetts General Hospital for Children.

References

[i] Isaiah 55:2 King James Version, Bible Gateway.
http://www.biblegateway.com/passage/?search=Isaiah+55%3A2&version=KJV

[ii] "Sea Salt vs. Table Salt." American Heart Association.
September 11, 2013.
http://www.heart.org/HEARTORG/Conditions/HighBloodPressure/PreventionTreatmentofHighBloodPressure/Sea-Salt-Vs-Table-Salt_UCM_430992_Article.jsp

[iii] Alleman, Gayle, A., M.S.,R.D. "Ultimate Guide to Vinegar."
How Stuff Works. http://recipes.howstuffworks.com/how-vinegar-works1.htm

[iv] "History of Parmesan Cheese." Parmesan.Com.
http://www.parmesan.com/history/history-of-parmesan-cheese/

[v] Cassidy, Frederic, G. "Among the Old Words." American
Speech, Vol. 55, No. 4 (Winter, 1980), pp. 295-297. Duke
University Press. Retrieved from
http://dlbdl1ube5d16t0pd2eyvv7fn-wpengine.netdna-ssl.com/among-the-old-words-Read-AmSpeech-1980.pdf

[vi] CD Triggers: Mayo Clinic. www.mayoclinic.com/health/celiac-disease/ds00319/DSECTION=causes

[vii] "The Mediterranean Diet." Oldways – Health Through
Heritage.   http://oldwayspt.org/resources/heritage-pyramids/mediterranean-pyramid/overview

[viii] Gulli, Cathy. "The Dangers of Going Gluten Free," MacLean's
Magazine. September 10, 2013

[ix] Bennett, Patrick. "Is Gluten Content to Blame for the Rise of

Celiac Disease?".
https://www.allergicliving.com/2013/09/16/is-gluten-content-to-blame-for-the-rise-of-celiac-disease/

[x] Celiac Disease: About Celiac Disease Canadian Celiac Association. http://www.celiac.ca/index.php/about-celiac-disease-2/symptoms-treatment-cd/

[xi] Marshall, Lee. "Gluten Intolerance: "Gluten Free Not Just A Fad for Some." CBC News. May 1, 2013. www.cbc.ca/news/health/gluten-free-not-just-a-fad-for-some-1.1307108/

[xii] "20 ppm." Canadian Celiac Association. CCA eNews online edition. Newsletter to subscription members posted online, September 2013.

[xiii] Villi: Filed under: "Causes." Mayo Clinic Staff, author. Mayo Clinic. www.mayoclinic.com/health/celiac-disease/DS00319/DSECTION=causes.

[xiv] Lymphocytic Colitis: Filed under: "Definition." Mayo Clinic Staff, author. Mayo Clinic www.mayoclinic.com/health/microscopic-colitis/DS00824

[xv] Glycemic Index: Filed under: Nutrition & Healthy Eating: "Glycemic Index: What's Behind The Claims." Mayo Clinic Staff, author. Mayo Clinic. http://www.mayoclinic.com/health/glycemic-index-diet/MY00770

[xvi] "Eating Raw Garlic Can Prevent Cancer, Study Suggests. https://www.cbc.ca/news/health/eating-raw-garlic-can-prevent-cancer-study-suggests-1.1343422

[xvii] Paravantes, Elena. "The Mediterranean Diet and Metabolic Syndrome." https://www.oliveoiltimes.com/health-news/mediterranean-diet-metabolic-syndrome/13715